Praise for Live These Words

Everyone I know longs to step up to new levels of trust and confidence in God, but how do we begin? In *Live These Words*, my friend Lucinda McDowell has constructed a staircase of 40 key steps to help us to new heights of spiritual intimacy—through life experiences, solid biblical lessons, stellar quotations and prayers. Convicting, yet comforting. I highly recommend this book!

ca **Joni Eareckson Tada**, *Joni and Friends*
International Disability Center

Lucinda's are clear, practical words, delightfully added to the always-needed contemplative conversation that advises us to *be* with God so that we can better *do* for God.

ca **Robert Benson**, author of
Dancing on the Head of a Pen

My friend Cindy's book, *Live These Words,* has all the imprints of her personality—profound, really smart, funny, and real. It will scoop you up into the wonder of His Word and give you forty days of encouragement and direction on living it. Then, my guess is that you'll be hooked, and your forty-day journey will turn into a lifetime.

ca **Jennifer Kennedy Dean**, author of
Live a Praying Life

Words matter. And they don't have to be many or long to do so. Cindy McDowell has selected some of the key words of our faith and put them in settings and stories that are truly encouraging and positive. In fact, I am passing on two chapters to my grandchildren because they are so encouraging for where they are right now. Take one of these "words" daily—for your spiritual health.

ca **Dr. Leighton Ford**, president of Leighton Ford
Ministries and author of *The Attentive Life*

Live these words, pray these words, trust these words, but most importantly read these words of Cindy's as part of your daily walk with our Lord.

ଔ **Debbie Macomber**, #1 *New York Times* bestselling author

In *Live These Words* you will be drawn deeper into God's truth and further into a contemplative devotional experience. The surprise in this book is that often the take-away will involve listening, waiting, meditating, or lingering over a single word, *before* leaping into action. Lucinda Secrest McDowell is a gifted communicator—both on the platform and in written form. Don't miss this book!

ଔ **Carol Kent**, director of *Speak Up* and author of *Unquenchable*

Most of us spend the majority of our waking hours exegeting the verbs *to do, to want,* and *to have*. We've filled our lives with incessant noise and activity but discover that our lives are actually rather unfulfilling and exhausting. Cindy invites us to exegete the verb *to be*, with encouraging words that breathe the abundant life of Christ into our souls.

ଔ **Dr. Stephen A. Macchia**, president of *Leadership Transformations* and author of *Crafting a Rule of Life*

Warmth, wisdom, and wonderful stories pave a path to active living that both lifts the soul and honors God. Perfect meditations for our tough times. Encouraging and hopeful. Two thumbs up!

ଔ **Patricia Raybon**, author of *I Told the Mountain to Move*

Do you need refreshment? Grab this book. You'll discover one word to focus on each day—a word illustrated with delightful stories and rich insights which will leave you longing for more. *Live These Words* is a great book to give to your friends!

ଔ **Susan Alexander Yates**, author of *And Then I Had Kids*

These action verbs from the Bible capture the reader's interest, and Lucinda Secrest McDowell's illustrations—stories from real life and the Bible, activities to try, and beautiful prayers—invite the reader to draw near to God in new ways. *Live These Words* is a wonderful guide for Lent or any 40-day period, making the life of faith seem doable, inviting, and deeply rewarding.

ぴ **Dr. Lynne M. Baab**, professor and author of
The Power of Listening

Reading these devotionals I had the feeling of being wrapped in a warm quilt of love and encouragement. The topics presented are thought provoking and timely for each of us who live busy lives. I love Cindy McDowell's writing style and you will be blessed as you *Live These Words* for the next forty days.

ぴ **Carole Lewis**, director emeritus *First Place 4 Health* and author of *A Thankful Heart*

How could I resist a book that starts with these words: "I spent half a lifetime trying to *do* enough for God. Enough that He would love me, accept me..."? No talking down to readers or attempts at sounding spiritual, she opens her heart and allows us to see her inner self—which enables us to see ourselves. Not only does the first sentence of *Live These Words* grab me, but Lucinda Secrest McDowell writes with three significant qualities: honesty, warmth, and practicality. Rarely do I find all three in the same book.

ぴ **Cecil Murphey,** author of 135 books, including, *Gifted Hands* and *90 Minutes in Heaven*

Take 40 days and fast from every worthless word in your thoughts, in your mouth, and on your mind. Substitute these words and you'll change your life. *Live These Words* is simply Cindy's best book ever. I love it!

ぴ **Virelle Kidder**, author of *Meet Me at the Well*

Live These Words is a book I will return to many times—and give to friends. There is power in Cindy's story-telling; a rich treasure of words and prayers from great women and men of faith both ancient and contemporary, and—above all—His

Words. Frederick Buechner tells us words make things happen: *Live These Words*!

ᔕ Linda Anderson, president of *Mom to Mom*, board of *Gordon Conwell Theological Seminary*

Live These Words helps believers do just that: apply the Bible so we can grow deeper with God. Written by a master storyteller who delights in sharing funny and touching stories, this 40-day guide gives you practical steps for making God's Word real and truly applicable to whatever challenging situations you face each day.

ᔕ Dr. Jennifer Degler, psychologist and author of *No More Christian Nice Girl*

Spending time in God's Word is a given in the lives of most Christians, but after we've done some studying, meditating, and praying, what's next? In *Live These Words*, Lucinda Secrest McDowell motivates us to get up out of our reading chairs and make a difference. Her meaty, diverse, and challenging explorations of imperatives from the Bible are a call to action that will transform our relationship with God and redefine the interactions we have with the people He brings into our lives.

ᔕ Lauren Yarger, author event producer, *TheWritePros.com*

Live These Words by Lucinda Secrest McDowell is my kind of devotional—deep but practical. I need that! These devotionals are also personal and reader-friendly, meaning that I'm encouraged but not intimidated by them. And the forty-day length is perfect!

ᔕ Kathi Macias, author of *The 40-Day Devotional Challenge*

Live These Words will help you both sit and stand. Sit quietly with God and enjoy stories that will help action verbs come alive. Then stand up and take steps for those actions to take form in your life.

ᔕ Anne Grizzle, author of *Reminders of God*

Thank you, Cindy, for *Live These Words*. I know you have invested in the Kingdom by personally living the words of our Heavenly Father for many years, and now through this book, many of us are encouraged to do the same.

> ∝ Kendra Smiley, author of *Live Free*

Lucinda Secrest McDowell skillfully shares how to walk the balance between *being with* God and *doing for* God. Using memoir, biblical stories, and fascinating profiles, *Live These Words* takes us on a journey of exploring some powerful action verbs from the Bible and then helps us actually do something with them. I am so pleased to find a devotional book that inspires a daily response.

> ∝ Georgia Shaffer, psychologist and author of *Avoiding the 12 Relationship Mistakes Women Make*

Lucinda McDowell's *Live These Words* challenges the reader to move from head knowledge into obedience through a beautiful blend of *being* and *doing*. An encouraging gem of a devotional that draws you closer to Jesus.

> ∝ Tessa Afshar, author of *Pearl in the Sand*

Words matter. For decades I have personally known and observed how Cindy McDowell has deepened through her very unique life-journey. She has given us the best choice of words by skillfully, with vulnerability, weaving scripture, her story, and that of others in a way that makes following Christ practical and life altering. Gratefully, each chapter concludes with deep prayers from the ages that can spark a new and vital interest in going deeper into Christlikeness. Crawl into each word with the anticipation of being renewed in thought and action and don't miss *Live These Words!*

> ∝ Gail MacDonald, author of *In His Everlasting Arms*

With insight like fresh linen, Lucinda graciously invites us to live the Word of God not merely read it. These forty days will refresh your spirit and encourage your heart.

> ∝ Gari Meacham, author of *Spirit Hunger*

Live These Words contains so many gifts for the reader; gems of wisdom, wonderful stories, and experiences are ribboned through every paragraph. Don't be in a hurry. Relax into each day's teaching. Do the thinking. Take the time to let these readings wash over you, changing you, allowing you to tap into that grace that can never be earned. Simultaneously meaty and accessible, this is a thoughtful and beautiful book.

ca Carol Barnier, author of *Engaging Today's Prodigal*

Lucinda's book *Live These Words - an active response to God*, is a 40-day devotional reading with depth. In each reading, highlighted words of Scripture are deliciously presented, savored, and afterwards, a sweet aftertaste lingers that compels us to action.

ca Leslie Vernick, counselor and author
of *The Emotionally Destructive Relationship*

I reserve a special section on my bookshelves for titles by Lucinda Secrest McDowell. Each of her works is well-researched, thoughtfully expressed and deeply felt. *Live These Words* is no exception. Get one for yourself and another for a friend who needs the encouragement of the living faith Cindy's writing reflects.

ca Maggie Wallem Rowe, M.A.B.S., speaker,
author, and dramatist

Cindy McDowell's new book *Live These Words* brings the Bible alive for readers every day. Written with grace and a deep understanding of truth, *Live These Words* is a must-read.

-Cheri Fuller, author of *The One Year Praying the Promises of God*

Luminous. Practical. Engaging. With a lovely touch, Lucinda enlightens biblical imperatives with a sensitivity that meets our deepest desires. For our own souls, Lucinda prompts us to hope in God, not worry, and pray continually. For our relationships, she encourages us to lavishly love, forgive, and give to one another. These forty devotional readings remind us that following the

Bible's simple advice fosters a sacred, loving, meaningful life. I plan to keep *Live These Words* on my nightstand for daily guidance and inspiration.

ca Judith Couchman, author of
Designing a Woman's Life

Words! There are just over one million words in the English language and Lucinda has captured the essence and energy of 40 transforming words! Through her personal reflection, practical application, and prayerful guidance, these words have come to rest in my heart and change my life. Read this book, *live these words*, and know Him in a deeper and richer way.

ca Dr. Cynthia Fantasia, pastor,
Grace Chapel, Lexington MA

Cindy Secrest McDowell has written a unique and dynamic devotional. Through her warm storytelling style, she lovingly shows us how to incorporate God's action verbs into our Christian life. *Live These Words* contains words of life, instruction, and hope—all beautifully written and applicable to anyone who wants to grow their relationship with the Savior.

ca Grace Fox, author of *Morning Moments with God*

Vulnerable or strong, nurturing or longing, this wise women shares what God has taught her so far. On your own journey, *Live These Words* will put a sparkle in your eye and a spring in your step, offering very specific ways to live out your faith.

ca Dr. Miriam Adeney, author of *Kingdom Without Borders*
and board of *Christianity Today*

Lucinda's wisdom in *Live These Words* is profound, personal, and practical. Time spent with her is always rich and with each page, each moment you feel you are becoming a better person.

ca Pam Farrel, author of
Devotions for Women on the Go

Lucinda Secrest McDowell unpacks 40 words that matter from God's Word. With her, we travel with Abram, pour out the last oil with the widow, climb a contemporary mountain, and celebrate life's gifts, even in the midst of challenge. I found these stories becoming my stories, our stories, woven together with words of wisdom and prayers of well-known pilgrims who have preceded us. Through these words, we are invited to take the next step —that's all God asks of us: take the next step. Do we dare *live these words?*

ଔ Dr. Marta D. Bennett, pastor and professor, International Leadership University, Nairobi, Kenya

Living life according to God's Word is the secret to joy and contentment and Cindy McDowell provides an easy-to-follow format for discovering these truths. *Live These Words* is a perfect tool to use for your daily quiet time with the Lord.

ଔ Nancy McGuirk, author of *To Live is Christ - Philippians*

Live These Words is an encouraging, deep, thoughtful, practical tool. While we are acclaimed for our hard work for God's sake, we are rarely affirmed for our resting. We need both. Lucinda writes with insight and imagery and her intriguing use of original language adds depth to the readings and to common, often overused and little understood concepts in faith circles. An excellent journey that will change the way you live.

ଔ Jane Rubietta, author of *Finding Life – From Eden to Gethsemene*

I highly recommend *Live These Words* because it holds truth, wisdom, and grace for anyone who desires a daily faithful walk with God. I love the prayers from many older and contemporary writers and have been helped by Cindy's clear and very practical writing.

ଔ Valerie Elliot Shepard, author of *Pilipinto's Happiness*

As I read *Live These Words*, I kept thinking: *Oh I really love this day's wisdom, this word Cindy is focusing on, this perfect quote, this personal story, this quickening prayer. This is the best one!* Then I thought that again with the next day's reading. I hope our intimate God will use this inspiring book in the same way with you.

ca Jane Van Antwerp, children's author of
Big Jesus and *If We Could See Prayer*

Jesus said that if we love Him, we'll obey His commands—but sometimes just the thought is overwhelming! There are so many things we feel we could or should be doing. Lucinda Secrest McDowell teaches us to focus on one word—one command—each day. What a practical, powerful, life-changing way to walk in obedience and grow deeper in our relationship with Him.

ca Christin Ditchfield, author of *A Way with Words*

"Live a life worthy of the Lord and please Him in every way, bearing fruit in every good work, growing in the knowledge of God" (Colossians 1:10). Lucinda Secrest McDowell inspires and encourages us to do so with the beautiful words contained in her delightful book. *Live These Words* is a great pick-me-up for the busy woman or man.

ca Susan Wales, executive producer of
The Annual Movieguide® Awards

Most words wash over us with little effect. But some words are worth catching, pondering, and letting them influence the way we live. In *Live These Words*, Cindy catches a few weighty words from the Bible for us in a way that is interesting, informative, uplifting, and devotionally helpful.

ca Dr. Don Sweeting, President, Reformed Theological
Seminary, Orlando

Live These Words is a lot like the author, Cindy—full of deep reflective insight and practical creativity. Springboarding off the action verbs of Scripture, she dives into ancient prayers, contemplative reflections, psalms, hymns, and contemporary stories to energize our daily lives with these words of life. This book will help the action-oriented live from a deeper, richer motivation and connection with Jesus and will motivate the contemplatives to get in the race and do it!

ca Lael Arrington, author of *A Faith and Culture Devotional*

Live These Words

Live These Words

an active response to God

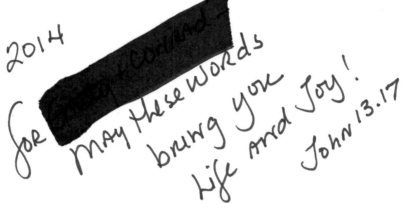

Handwritten inscription:
2014
for ██████ + Conrad ~
May these Words bring you
Life And Joy!
John 13.17

Lucinda Secrest McDowell

Signature: Lucinda Secrest McDowell

Bold Vision Books
PO Box 2011
Friendswood, Texas 77549

Copyright © Lucinda Secrest McDowell, 2014

ISBN # 978-09912842-3-8

Library of Congress LCCN: 2014936926

Published in the United States of America.

Bold Vision Books
PO Box 2011
Friendswood, Texas 77549
www.boldvisionbooks.com

Interior design by kae Creative Solutions
Edited by Katie McDivitt
Cover Photo © Cappui | Dreamstime
Author Photo by Carl Cramer Pho   CarlCramer.com

Bible Version Information and permissions
on page 276

dedication

Dedicated to
all my children
and grandchildren

These teachings are not empty words;
they are your very *life*.

Deuteronomy 32:47

Table of Contents

Come to Me, all you who are weary and burdened, and I will give you rest. Matthew 11:28

Trust in Him at all times, you people; pour out your hearts to Him, for God is our refuge. Psalm 62:8

Hope in God; for I shall again praise Him, my help and my God. Psalm 43:5 NRSV

Fear not, for I am with you; Be not dismayed, for I am your God. I will strengthen you, Yes, I will help you, I will uphold you with My righteous right hand. Isaiah 41:10 NKJV

...pour oil into all the jars.... 2 Kings 4:4

day 6   60

pray

...pray all the time; thank God no matter what happens. This is the way God wants you who belong to Christ Jesus to live. 1 Thessalonians 5:17 THE MESSAGE

day 7   65

wash

...wash yourself seven times in the Jordan, and your flesh will be restored and you will be cleansed. 2 Kings 5:10

day 8   71

go

Go from your country, your people and your father's household to the land I will show you. Genesis 12:1

day 9   76

call

Call to Me and I will answer you and tell you great and unsearchable things you do not know. Jeremiah 33:3

day 10   82

wait

Wait for the LORD; be strong, and let your heart take courage; wait for the LORD! Psalm 27:14 NRSV

day 11

praise   89

Praise the LORD, my soul, and never forget all the good He has done. Psalm 103:2 GW

day 18
forget
Forget the former things; do not dwell on the past.
Isaiah 43:18

day 19
sing
Sing to the LORD a new song, for He has done
marvelous things…. Psalm 98:1

day 20
forgive
…forgive one another if any of you has a grievance
against someone. Forgive as the Lord forgave you.
Colossians 3:13

day 21
proclaim
…proclaim the message; be persistent whether the
time is favorable or unfavorable; convince, rebuke,
and encourage, with the utmost patience in teaching.
2 Timothy 4:2 NRSV

day 22
receive
…receive power when the Holy Spirit comes on
you…. Acts 1:8

day 23
give
Give, and it will be given to you. A good measure,
pressed down, shaken together and running over,
will be poured into your lap. Luke 6:38

day 24   164
clothe
...clothe yourselves with compassion, kindness, humility, gentleness and patience. Colossians 3:12

day 25   170
work
...work enthusiastically for the Lord, for you know that nothing you do for the Lord is ever useless. 1 Corinthians 15:58 NLT

day 26   175
ask
...ask for the ancient paths, ask where the good way is, and walk in it, and you will find rest for your souls. Jeremiah 6:16

day 27   181
weep
...weep with those who weep. Romans 12:15 ESV

day 28   186
welcome
...welcome strangers into your home. By doing this, some people have welcomed angels as guests, without even knowing it. Hebrews 13:2 CEV

day 29   191
remember
Remember the days of old; consider the generations long past. Ask your father and he will tell you, your elders, and they will explain to you.
Deuteronomy 32:7

day 30   199
look
Look to the LORD and His strength; seek His face always. 1 Chronicles 16:11

day 31   204
choose
… choose life, so that you and your children may live and that you may love the LORD Your God, listen to His voice, and hold fast to Him.
Deuteronomy 30:19-20

day 32   209
leave
Leave all your worries with Him, because He cares for you. 1 Peter 5:7 GNT

day 33   214
shine
…shine like stars in the dark world.
Philippians 2:15 NCV

day 34   219
consider
…consider others as more important than yourselves. Everyone should look out not only for his own interests, but also for the interests of others.
Philippians 2:3-4 HCSB

gratitudes

Thank you to the many family and friends who encouraged me in the writing of *Live These Words*, but also—and more importantly—in the *living* of these words in my own life. Though you may not see your name here, you know who you are.

I'm especially grateful for a few days away in places of sanctuary where I could be still and listen to God's voice. A special thanks for the gracious hospitality of Newt and Barbara for "Mountain Meadows," Monty and Anne for "Dover Shore," Jim and Karen for "Riven Rock," Nick and Euphanel for "Round Top Retreat," and Don and Judy for "Singing Hills." Those five far-flung places in the Connecticut Berkshires, the Washington San Juan Islands, the New York Adirondacks, the Texas countryside, and the New Hampshire mountains always inspire me.

There are several affinity groups who strongly undergirded me with prayer and practical helps throughout this particular book project. Special thanks to my SpaSisters, my Tuesday night Women's Bible Study, my New England Christian Writers Retreat community, the awesome AWSAs, and my couples Growth Group.

Hugs to my best friend Maggie R., my sisters Cathy and Susan, and my mother Sarah who each read the very early stages of my manuscript and said they thought it would be my best book (I think they say that every time, but it still meant a lot.)

Thanks to publishers George and Karen Porter, and the whole team at Bold Vision Books for helping launch my words out into the world. Yes, we are kindred spirits.

And a special note of gratitude to the many friends and colleagues in ministry who agreed to read my little book and offer words of endorsement before publication. (I asked so many because I wasn't sure anyone would say yes.) I know that each of you is even busier than I am, so I am doubly grateful you would do me this honor. Thanks Anne, Carol B., Carol K., Carole L., Cec, Cheri, Christin, Cynthia, Debbie, Don, Gail, Gari, Georgia, Grace, Jane R., Jane V., Jennifer D., Jennifer K. D., Joni, Judith, Kathi, Kendra, Lael, Lauren, Leighton, Leslie, Linda, Lynne, Maggie R., Marta, Miriam, Nancy, Pam, Patricia, Robert, Steve, Susan W., Susan Y., Tessa, Val, and Virelle.

What would I have done without my local writers group—who advised and edited and prayed and then advised, edited and prayed some more? We are an eclectic trio, but somehow manage to balance out each other in whatever is needed at the time— whether it be book launches, road trips, or chocolate. This book would never have been written without the support of Lauren and Tessa—so thanks, friends.

Thank you to my children—Justin, Tim, Fiona, Tim K., Maggie and Stephen—for helping me *live these words* in an atmosphere of grace and joy. I know your mama often says and does things that perhaps make you wonder, but just think, I could be dull and predictable! May each of you know that I love you the world and dedicate all I have written in here to you and yours.

To my husband, Mike, may I say Happy 30th Anniversary this month! I want everyone to know that I would never have been able to *live* a single one of these words without your loyal support and faithful prayers. You continue to be God' gift to my life and there's no one I'd rather have by my side on this exhilarating journey. I love you always.

Finally. To God who is my Heavenly Father, to Jesus who is the Lover of my Soul, and to the Holy Spirit who is my Power and Nudger—I'm Yours and always will be, through grace alone, now and forever.

*The magic of words is that they have power
to do more than convey meaning;
not only do they have the power to
make things clear, they make things happen.*

Frederick Buechner

introduction

There are two kinds of Christian living.
One is a life of activity.
The other is the contemplative life.
These two lives are united.
It is impossible to live the one without
having some of the other.

ჽ Anonymous, *The Cloud of
Unknowing,* 14th century[1]

being and doing

I spent half a lifetime trying to *do* enough for God. Enough that He would love me, accept me, and find me worthy to share in His kingdom work.

But I could never quite get it right.

No matter how much my striving accomplished, my faltering and failing seemed to cancel out the achievement. I was once again cast upon His mercy, feeling defeated and discouraged.

Many years ago, God took me through a "grace tutorial"—teaching me how to accept grace as His free gift, one that I can never earn and never lose.

Though I carried the gift around for years, I had never appropriated it into my life. When I finally opened the gift of grace, I was released from being a P.O.W.—prisoner of works. God reached down to me in my pit of *doing for* Him (the Hebrew word for grace implies "to stoop") and lifted me into a place of *being with* Him.

Resting in His care. Soaking up His strength. Listening to His voice. Gaining wisdom from His Word. Out of such tender healing, I was able to do more, to serve others from a place of security and sanctuary, instead of striving for success.

More and more I long for the contemplative life.

My early morning hour in prayer and reading and singing could easily go on much longer if I didn't have such ordinary things to do such as go to work, clean house, prepare food, and interact with people. I draw strength, wisdom, guidance, nourishment, and so much more from times of *being* in the presence of my heavenly Father.

But that same loving Father doesn't actually want me to just sit at His feet all day.

He fills me up for the very purpose that I might pour myself out. My *doing* comes out of my *being*. Both are necessary and required for the Christ-follower.

Jesus told His disciples, "Now that you know these things, you will be blessed if you do them" (John 13:17). Knowing is foundational. Not just knowing the facts, but knowing God. So, yes, we absolutely must first and foremost invest in our commitment to knowing God. And there is no better way for that to happen than through prayer, silence, worship, fasting, solitude, Bible reading—the "ancient path."

But in order to receive the blessing, we must then *act* on our knowledge. As John Bunyan said in *Pilgrim's Progress*, "Talkers and boasters enjoy knowing something. God is pleased when it is done."

Throughout Scripture we find words that call us to be proactive—fear not, shine, pray, trust, encourage, forgive, praise, look, persevere, and more. It's not enough for me to love God and *know* what He wants; I need to actively respond.

In the doing, I am not only blessed, but allowed to live a full life that influences others for the kingdom of God.

Perhaps you, like me, often wonder what God would have you do each day. Why not ask Him?

In my morning devotions, invariably I am directed to a word that both challenges and excites me as I pray over how I can make it real in my own life. Sometimes the opportunity to follow through appears quickly and other times it takes me quite a while to figure out how to do what God requests.

My prayers often include this ancient entreaty: *O Lord, mercifully receive the prayers of your people who call upon you, and grant that they may know and understand what things they ought to do, and also may have grace and power faithfully to accomplish them; through Jesus Christ, Amen. (*Book of Common Prayer*).*[2]

These days I ask God to give me at least one action verb as I daily read the Bible, the Psalms, my hymnal and prayer book. Then it is up to me to do something about it.

Believers back in the sixteenth century were encouraged by Ignatius of Loyola to gaze at the figure of Christ hanging on the cross and ask themselves these questions:

⁞   What have I done for Christ?

⁞   What am I doing for Christ?

⁞   What ought I to do for Christ?

This book suggests that you spend the next forty days embracing and responding to some of God's richest, life-giving words.

Out of the being will come the doing. As you and I approach these words with grace and humility, I suspect God will weave them beautifully into our own unique stories.

And then the blessing will follow.

Lucinda Secrest McDowell
"Sunnyside"
Wethersfield, Connecticut, USA

day 1

come

COME to Me, all you who are
weary and burdened, and
I will give you rest.
Matthew 11:28

I love sending out invitations.

In fact, one of the best parts of hosting an event is the opportunity to create a special invitation, beckoning others to come. Such invites need to be gracious, reflecting a style that fits the occasion, and always conveying the desire for another's company. But the recipient must never forget the reminder to *respondez s'il vous plait* (R.S.V.P.) —how else can the host be prepared with seating, food, and favors?

I also love receiving invitations from other people. I'm happy to open e-vites online, and I totally get saving money on postage, not to mention saving trees. However, call me old-fashioned or politically incorrect, but I still prefer being able to hold an invitation in my hand and post it on the fridge. Those tangibles make me less inclined to forget to respond.

As long as you invite me, I don't mind if it's by carrier pigeon.

Our word today—*come*—is an invitation from none other than Jesus Christ, one that definitely requires a response.

Yet I am amazed that so few who have read this invitation—to the "weary and burdened"—actually follow through to spend time with the Creator and Sustainer of the universe.

Including me.

We rationalize that once we have cleared our current schedule, or finished our work project, or raised all our kids...then maybe we will go to Jesus. But the price we pay for procrastinating is all too costly—alienation, deep soul hunger, loss of meaning, fear, stress, confusion, and so much more.

For those who do choose to take Jesus up on His invitation to bask in His presence, the take-home favor is out of this world—*rest*. We can fully rest in the assurance of His constant love for us and knowledge that He longs for us to draw near and spend time with Him simply because He created us.

Most of all, God provides for us something in short supply these days—a safe place.

Who wouldn't want that? Are you afraid of what might be revealed during a quiet, restful time in the presence of your Lord? Could it simply be easier to fill life with busyness so that the hard stuff never has to be faced or dealt with?

It is only in the silence that we hear the voice of God speaking directly to our souls.

Perhaps He will reveal areas that need change or healing. Perhaps He will plant the seed of a dream you never thought attainable. Most probably He will whisper words of love and affirmation and encouragement in your ear. And you will be strengthened for what is ahead.

Last summer my husband, Mike, and I accepted an invitation to house/pet sit for dear friends who live out in the country a few hours away. Because Mike was also on sabbatical, we responded "yes" to spending those days enveloped in the rest and love of Jesus. We daily awakened with open hands to receive what God had for us in such an absolutely beautiful setting. With no real responsibilities (other than a dear black Labrador retriever named Ben), we read, we prayed, we walked, we listened, we ate, we wrote, we breathed. And then, once daily, we took a fun outing together.

Yet we almost didn't even make it there as Mike was all for reneging on our commitment at the last minute. He felt that packing and arranging to be out of town seemed overwhelming after some recent challenges in our life. But I reminded him that we had already R.S.V.P.'d and couldn't get out of it.

Soon after arriving and settling in, he thanked me for that push.

There at "Mountain Meadows," I settled into an antique wicker chaise on the screen porch which beckoned me during each morning cup of coffee. As I sat back and listened to the singing birds, the chirping cicada, and occasional patter of raindrops, I was content.

I was with God.

Just like Piglet in *Winnie the Pooh* as he seeks his dearest friend.

> Piglet sidled up to Pooh from behind.
> "Pooh?" he whispered.
> "Yes, Piglet?"
> "Nothing," said Piglet, taking Pooh's hand.
> "I just wanted to be sure of you."[3]

Do you need to just "be sure" of Jesus? Then, get right next to Him.

One day His disciples excitedly gathered around Him to report all they had done and taught through His power. It was a busy time because so many people were coming and going that they did not even have a chance to eat.

But Jesus knew they had needs not yet recognized, so he responded, "... 'Come with me by yourselves to a quiet place and get some rest.' So they went away by themselves in a boat to a solitary place" (Mark 6:31-32).

In this particular instance, the disciples' quiet time with their Master was short-lived. But it proved enough to provide great power for the next event. As the throngs discovered them, they, too, gathered around Jesus and soon grew hungry. What followed was the feeding of the five thousand.

From rest to strength; from strength to miracles.

Each of us has received the same invitation to "come" from Jesus. What are we waiting for?

Softly and tenderly Jesus is calling, Calling for you and for me; See, on the portals He's waiting and watching, Watching for you and for me. Come home, come home, You who are weary, come home; Earnestly, tenderly, Jesus is calling, Calling, O sinner, come home![4]

live these words

When did you last set apart a time somewhere to simply be in God's presence? Perhaps you have never made arrangements for such an experience. Why not start today by exploring a quiet place and marking a specific time on your calendar? Convents and monasteries usually offer such day retreat options to people in the community. Some churches have facilities appropriate for escaping the busyness of the outside world and all your responsibilities. Or you might want to do a home exchange with a friend—somehow we aren't as distracted by chores while staying in someone else's home. Whatever you do, enter into your time with an open heart to receive God's love.

Come with open ears to hear His voice and come with open hands to carry back all you have gained. Just *come*.

pray these words

Father, I exult in the free, confident access You have provided so that I can come into Your Presence for warm fellowship, for refreshment, for mercy when I've failed, for grace when I'm in need. What a joy to know that I can draw near to You at any moment, wherever I may be... that I can come boldly to Your throne of grace, assured of Your glad welcome. Thank You that I can 'be still' and know that You are God... that You are in control... and that I can restfully depend upon You and absorb Your strength and joy and peace. To think that You not only permit me to come before You but You actually desire my fellowship, my worship, my prayers and my eternal presence! Thank You. Amen.

                       ℘ Ruth Myers (1928-2010)[5]

day 2

trust

TRUST in Him at all times, you people; pour
out your hearts to Him, for God is our refuge.
Psalm 62:8

I looked up at Daddy with wide-eyed, ten-year-old
amazement. "I can't believe you burned down Brookside."

The fire had left its devastation—everything around
us was black and charred. There were no tall grasses left,
no bushes, no wildflowers. Brookside was our family's
small farm just outside of town, a place where we fished,
hunted, played, rode horses, and spent campouts at the
cabin christened by my parents as "The Last Resort."

"Oh, Cindygirl, I didn't burn down Brookside,"
Daddy replied with a grin. "This is what is called controlled
burning—setting carefully guarded fires to clean out
the underbrush and make way for new spring growth.
Remember, I'm a forester. This is what we foresters do
every year."

I wanted to trust Daddy, to believe that what he said was indeed the truth. But the blackened ground didn't look like it would ever see green again. It seemed more reasonable to trust what my eyes saw instead of what my ears heard. Tentatively, I sought to grasp what he had said. "So, it only *looks* like you destroyed Brookside, but what you were really doing is preparing it for growing?"

"Exactly," Daddy explained. "Those weeds and tall grasses would have choked back the new plants and flowers coming this spring. So we clear that away, and before you know it, this whole area will once again be covered in beautiful green."

For another moment I experienced an internal battle between what the person I trusted was saying and what I was actually seeing.

I knew that my daddy loved this farm, that he enjoyed walking through the trails and boating on the two ponds and driving the jeep from the brooks that bordered each side of the vast acreage. I also knew that he was a tree planter as well as a forester, that he always replenished the lands that provided wood for his pulpwood business.

Most of all, I knew that he was a person I could believe with all my heart. I chose to trust him because I knew him so well.

And my trust was rewarded with visible evidence—by the very next weekend there were tiny shoots of green peeking up all over the farm.

The psalmist in today's verse admonishes us to *trust* God at all times because He is our refuge, our "safe place." When we are young children, our parents should embody the same kind of safety, refuge, and trustworthiness as our heavenly Father. In my life, I was privileged to make an easy transition from trusting a trustworthy father to trusting my heavenly Father. But sadly, we know that is not always the case.

How can we live out the word *trust* when others have betrayed our trust so many times that we have become wary and reticent?

In this verse, the word *trust* is translated from the Hebrew word *chacah*, a verb which means "to seek refuge or put trust in God." Its noun form, *machacah*, is actually interchangeable with our English word refuge. So when we speak of trust, we are also speaking of a safe place to dwell, actually living in a refuge of trust.

One missionary reminds us how God is that safe, strong place: "Thank You, Lord, that Your name is a strong tower where I can be safe and encouraged. You are my Rock, my Refuge, and my Rescuer.... As one of Your loved ones, I can rest in Your arms; I can lie down in safety, close to You, assured that You protect me all night long as well as all day long. What promises and privileges are mine!"[6]

As my childhood story suggests, one of the stumbling blocks in trusting is that trust involves saying no to our natural tendencies and yes to what sometimes appears impossible. That's where faith comes in.

In his helpful handbook *Everything You Always Wanted to Know About God*, Eric Metaxas reminds us that "Faith means having trust in something.... God doesn't want people to trust in 'whatever' and take dumb risks. He wants people to trust in Him, because He's utterly real and utterly trustworthy. If He isn't real and worthy of our trust, we'd be fools to have faith in Him. The object of our faith must be worthy of our faith."[7]

My father was a worthy object of my trust, so I chose to believe what he said instead of what I mistakenly deduced from my surroundings. I could wholeheartedly put my trust in him because I knew his heart. "If you know who God is, you will want to turn your will over to Him, because you trust Him with your life, you trust that His plans for you are far better even than the plans you've made for yourself. But if you don't really believe that God is the loving and wonderful God of the Bible who knows you intimately and loves you passionately, you'll never feel free to trust Him with your life."[8]

What do you see when you look at your life today? Is there devastation? Have dreams been shattered? Are resources depleted? It's pretty easy to trust what you see as the final reality.

But you might be wrong.

The burnt–out brush of your life right now might very well be a carefully controlled burning orchestrated by your heavenly Father to provide ideal conditions for new growth. Maybe something in your life has to go so that God can replace it with something even better.

Will you *trust* Him to do that in His way and His time?

live these words

I know you have probably been betrayed by someone you once trusted. It hurt. You were transparent, vulnerable, and had expected them to keep confidences. But instead, they judged and ridiculed you, or they revealed your secrets. Once we've been hurt, we are wary and begin to build walls for protection. But that's not the way God wants His people to live. He wants to be our refuge, our safe place, where we truly can be authentic without risking criticism. Can you entrust yourself into God's hands today?

Years ago Mike and I left our home in the mountains —"High Hopes"—and moved to Virginia by the shore. We named our new home "Trust Haven" and believed God would do for us what He promised in Nahum 1:7,

> The Lord is good, a refuge in times of trouble.
> He cares for those who trust in Him....

All we wanted was for our home to be a refuge. It never occurred to us that we would have *times of trouble* there. Our year at "Trust Haven" was full of challenges that tested our trust. Still, we felt the house name was not a mistake.[9]

Write down three things/people you need to entrust to God today. Then, by faith, do it because "He cares for those who trust in Him."

pray these words

Dear heavenly Father, I praise you today for the multiple commands in the Bible to trust you. Father, first of all, for the many attempts I make not to need you and to be my own savior—or at least a consulting partner to the Trinity, forgive me. Even though I assume I will only be able to trust you with ALL my heart on the Day when Jesus returns, I will trust you today with as much of my heart as I can possibly muster.

Father, for the broken circumstances I'd love to fix, I surrender, palms up to you. I know you well enough to realize that things are not as they appear to me, with my naked eye. Even when I try to look at some things with the eye of faith, I'm still smitten with astigmatism of the soul.... Father, as this day unfolds, I choose to lean on you, and not my understanding; I choose to step on the path of grace, and off the highway of my willfulness; I choose to acknowledge you, and stop trying to inform and coach you. Bring your heart, hand and hope to bear. So very Amen I pray, in Jesus' merciful and mighty name.

                                         ಬ Scotty Smith[10]

day 3

HOPE in God; for I shall again praise
Him, my help and my God.
Psalm 43:5 NRSV

If anyone had reason to be without hope, it was Peter.

Robust, outspoken, zealous follower-of-Christ Peter. The one who suggested monuments be built in order for God to get the glory He deserved. The one who was willing to step out and walk on water in pure obedience and love. The one who vowed that even if everyone else deserted the Master, *he* never would.

And the same one who, when events began their downward spiral, denied vehemently that he ever knew the man.

Oh yeah, he had become *that* guy. The fair-weather friend. The stab them in the back when they're not looking teammate. The all-talk-and-no-action guy.

And now it was too late.

His Lord had been delivered over to be crucified, and Peter's own desertion had contributed to a finality that was the very definition of hopelessness. In Matthew's account of Peter's denial, we discover that after hearing the rooster crow, he went out and wept bitterly (chapter 26). The Message translation says, "...he...cried and cried and cried."

We don't know where Peter spent that hopeless weekend, but I suspect his was a storm-tossed sojourn, a drowning of all that he had once known and held dear. He desperately needed hope, "...an anchor for the soul, firm and secure" (Hebrews 6:19).

How appropriate that the one who looked down and began to sink in the water is the same one who cried out during the storm, "Master, don't you care that we are drowning?" Peter who possibly spent an entire weekend drowning in tears of remorse and shame, found the hope that would become a new foundational anchor for his life so he might "again praise Him."

Because no matter how hopeless a situation appears, when God is in the middle of it, we can find hope.

Peter's hope began to emerge at an empty tomb on Sunday morning. In Mark's account (chapter 16), the angel startles Mary Magdalene, Mary the mother of Jesus, and Salome with the news that Christ is no longer in the tomb. "...tell His disciples and Peter, 'He is going on ahead of you into Galilee....'" God's messenger wanted to make sure the one who failed understood that the story wasn't over yet.

When his fishing for men ended so poorly, Peter had gone back to the life he knew before—fishing for fish. And Christ met him where he was. John (chapter 21) reports that Peter saw a man cooking breakfast on the shore and, recognizing the risen Master, he dove into the sea and swam to meet Him.

During their encounter, Jesus offered Peter three opportunities to reaffirm his commitment through grace, thus cancelling out his three denials.

"...do you love me?"

He [Peter] answered, "Yes, Lord, you know that I love you."

Jesus said, "Take care of my sheep."

Peter declares his love, not once but three times.

And Peter spent the rest of his life feeding the flock of new believers—preaching all that Christ had done for him, a sinner. I believe many were filled with hope as they realized that if God could use someone like Peter, he could also redeem their broken lives and give new purpose and meaning.

To his final days Peter encouraged others to "...set your hope fully on the grace that will be brought to you at the revelation of Jesus Christ" (1 Peter 1:13 ESV). His name had once been changed from Simon to *Cephas*, which means rock. And yet this human rock had crumbled under persecution and pressure.

What hope brought to Peter is a reminder that Christ's call to us, and His empowering of us to meet that call, can never fail, even though we can fail.

And now I'm going to tell you who you are, *really* are. You are Peter, a rock. This is the rock on which I will put together my church, a church so expansive with energy that not even the gates of hell will be able to keep it out (Matthew 16:18 THE MESSAGE).

If you are without hope today, will you remember the incredible ups and downs, ins and outs that were the life of Peter? Will you remember that although he faltered and failed, he eventually came back stronger than ever before to fulfill what God had called him to be so long ago—the strong rock?

Live as a person of hope today. No matter what you've done or not done.

Because *hope* is an anchor that holds fast.

live these words

It is said that human beings can live for forty days without food, four days without water, and four minutes without air. But we cannot live for four seconds without hope. Therefore, choosing to *hope* in God is not an option, but a necessity. Often we hear folks say things like "I hope it doesn't rain," or "I hope I got that job." But that kind of hope seems baseless. What we really need is a Source of hope, and our verse reminds that our Source is God. He is reliable, worthy, unchanging, and absolutely powerful.

Becky Pippert, in her book *Hope Has Its Reasons,* wrote "Christians are people of hope and not despair because we know that God, who had the first word, will have the last. He is never thwarted or caught napping by the circumstances of our lives."[11]

So today, where do you place your hope? If it is in institutions, they will fail you. If it is in the economy, you're in trouble. Even if your hope is based on a precious loved one, they, too, may let you down. Will you determine to place all your hopes and dreams and desires on God? He is truly able.

May the God of hope fill you with all joy and peace as you trust in Him, so that you may overflow with hope by the power of the Holy Spirit (Romans 15:13).

pray these words

O You Who Comes, Who are the hope of the world, give us hope. Give us hope that beyond the worst the world can do there is such a best that not even the world can take it from us, hope that none whom You have loved is ever finally lost, not even to death.

O You Who Died in loneliness and pain, suffer to die in us all that keeps us from You and from each other and from becoming as good and as brave as we are called to become. O Lamb of God, forgive us.

O You Who Rose Again, You Holy Spirit of Christ, arise and live within us now, that we may be Your body, that we may be Your feet to walk in the world's pain, Your hands to heal, Your heart to break, if need must be, for love of the world.

O Risen Christ, make Christs of us all. Amen.

ജ Frederich Buechner[12]

day 4

fear not

FEAR NOT, for I am with you; Be not
dismayed, for I am your God. I will
strengthen you, Yes, I will help you, I will
uphold you with My righteous right hand.
Isaiah 41:10 NKJV

*A*re you crazy?" I yelled at my professor who had just
told me to slowly back down a 100-foot cliff.

No matter that I was roped on belay (one end around
me and the other around him at the top). No matter that
this was part of my seminary course "Wilderness Training
for Spiritual Maturity." No matter that everyone else in
my class had already backed down the cliff and rappelled
(more like bounced) to the bottom.

I still thought he was crazy. And frankly, I was scared to death!

How could I be sure he had a firm grip on the rope or that it would truly hold me? How could I fling myself out over the edge when every instinct for self-preservation within me screamed otherwise? How could I overcome my fears and willingly walk backwards down a mountain?

I had to let go of control.

Repelling required a risk, trusting that the promised support would be there. I had to dig somewhere deep in my twenty-five-year-old wimpy self and find courage to go where I'd never gone before—to do what I'd never dared.

While repeatedly praying this promise, *He gives me hinds' feet to climb on the heights. He gives me hinds' feet to climb on the heights...* (my own quick version of Psalm 18), I closed my eyes, took a deep breath, and leapt backwards into the vast Adirondack wilderness with abandon.

Was it an act of courage? Was it an act of trust? Was it an act of desperation? Uh, yes. But with that one leap I experienced the God who grants courage to the fearful, the God who is always underneath with His everlasting arms, the God who promises to guide me in times of uncertainty.

This is the same God who, in fact, has faithfully walked with me for decades since that leap off the mountain.

He is the One who strengthens the fainthearted and supports the weak. In the intervening years, I have encountered far more frightening situations than my first foray into mountain climbing and rappelling—medical scares, unemployment, children's safety, financial challenges, and relationship loss. But the lessons are the same.

Trust in God's promises...and let go!

Did you know that there are more than 100 scriptures containing our word(s) for today—*fear not*? I suspect God said it so many times because He knows how prone we are to default into fear. Fear actually is one of the biggest obstacles to completely trusting and obeying what God says.

This emotion, which God hardwired into us originally as a self-protecting mechanism, was designed to be unpleasant enough to motivate us to take action and remove ourselves from the threat. In other words, to give the signal "fight or flight."

The word *fear* comes from an Old English word for danger. Fear would be a healthy emotion if it cropped up only when needed for real danger. But instead of motivating, fear often paralyzes because it attaches to what does not truly threaten us. We spend so much emotional energy feeding our fears, yet most of the things we fear actually never come to pass.

In today's scripture we are told to *fear not* because God is with us to help, strengthen, and uphold us. God covers all our weak, helpless, and failure fears.

A few chapters after today's verse, we are yet again promised God's presence through whatever we might encounter.

> ...Fear not, for I have redeemed you; I have called you by name; you are Mine. When you pass through the waters, I will be with you; and through the rivers, they shall not overflow you. When you walk through fire, you shall not be burned, Nor shall the flame scorch you. (Isaiah 43:1-2 NKJV).

When we are afraid, we can fully trust God with our fears. He is only a prayer away.

Max Lucado says, "Fear will always knock on your door. Just don't invite it in for dinner, and for heaven's sake don't offer it a bed for the night."[13]

There is a lot to fear in today's world. But we have a choice whether or not to open that door.

Let's stand with courage next to the Almighty God. Every time we face our fears instead of giving in, we are empowered for the next challenge.

I learned the power in facing fear a long time ago while hanging off a mountain, and it's stuck with me ever since.

live these words

Jesus asked His disciples during that fierce storm (Mark 4), "Why are you so afraid?" And I'll ask you the same thing, "What are your greatest fears?" Take some time to write them down. As you pray over the list, ask yourself why that particular fear has a hold on you and what promise from the Bible could you attach to alleviate it. Pray for deliverance and courage as you face your fears.

pray these words

Lord, I am afraid, so I ask for Your help in fighting my fear. Sometimes I don't quite know what I am afraid of. Fear of uncertainty, fear of failure, fear of being left on my own, fear of emptiness, fear of the unknown – these are the insecurities that attack me, particularly at night. At other times my fears are specific. They are anxieties about health, money, love, loneliness, and relationships. One or other of them always seems to be going wrong. Lord, I know I should trust You in such moments of fear. But my anxieties seem stronger than my trust. Help me to overcome my lack of confidence. Grant me the faith to know that the only true security comes from Your perfect love that casts out all fear. Through Jesus Christ our Lord, Amen.

ဆ Jonathan Aitken[14]

day 5

pour

...POUR oil into all the jars.... 2 Kings 4:4

*I*f you were down to your last morsel of food and God asked you to give it to Him, would you?

It seems the less we have, the more we want to cling to it.

In our economy, "almost nothing" is a desperate situation. However, in God's economy, "almost nothing" can actually end up being "exactly enough."

But only if we do what He says.

There was once a woman who faced such a dilemma. She was empty, with so many needs all around, yet with so little available to meet those needs—so little strength, money, time, resources. As the widow of one of the prophet Elisha's most faithful servants (2 Kings 4:1-7), she had suffered a triple blow: her husband died, the creditors were coming to take her children as slaves, and there was no food in the house. She was grieving, fearful, and destitute.

Perhaps you, too, are experiencing loss, fear, or financial ruin. In the middle of such deprivation, do you believe that God can truly bring something out of nothing?

The prophet Elisha came into this woman's home and asked how he could help, "What do you have in your house?" (verse 2).

And the widow answered "Your servant has nothing there at all...except a small jar of olive oil."

It's almost as though the one thing she had—the small jar of olive oil—was simply an afterthought because it seemed so ordinary, so insignificant. And yet, it was a start, a place for God, through His servant Elisha, to begin the miracle work.

I have often felt as though I had "nothing in the house...except" when it comes to what is needed for my daily life. Oh yeah, I have a lot of stuff around, but sometimes I'm down to bare bones when it comes to offering hope, offering wisdom, offering answers. That's when my answer needs to be, "I have nothing in the house except...my willingness to be used, Lord."

One of my favorite poems by Amy Carmichael, "Nothing in the House," begins with her telling God she has nothing in her house but pain. Amy, a Victorian-era missionary to India who rescued young girls from temple prostitution (early human trafficking), lived with chronic pain all her life. The last two verses of the poem are God's words to her:

> My servant, I have come into the house-
> I who know Pain's extremity so well
> That there can never be the need to tell

His power to make the flesh and
spirit quail:
Have I not felt the scourge, the thorn,
the nail?
And I, his Conqueror, am in the house,
Let not your heart be troubled:
do not fear:
Why shouldst thou, child of Mine,
if I am here?
My touch will heal thy song-bird's
broken wing,
And he shall have a braver song to sing.[15]

It is in the midst of our dire need that God makes
His presence known, but He also asks us to partner with
Him in remedying the situation. Are you empty? Do you
wonder how you can possibly have enough or be enough for
what is required from you?

Take a look at your resources—what has been
provided instead of what has been withheld. Even the
widow had something—one small jar of oil. And Elisha was
God's voice to ask her to do something with what she had.

God wants to do the same thing in my life and yours,
take something small and multiply it into more. But in the
process we may be asked to do some questionable things,
such as gathering more of nothing. Yes, Elisha immediately
told her to go and find as many empty jars as she could and
bring them into the house (verse 3).

What went through her mind as she was obeying
this strange request? What goes through your mind when
you are obeying God but not understanding His will and
His way? I confess I often grumble, "I'll do it, but it won't

make any difference," or "This is not the way the world works today, don't you know that, God?"

Then Elisha told her to take the one jar of oil and pour it all out into a house full of empty containers (verse 4). Perhaps she was secretly relieved he had told her to shut the doors so no neighbors would see her. And yet, as she poured, there was always more, more oil to fill every jar.

The impossible became possible.

And God's purposes for this widow's life—to enable her to become financially stable in order to provide for her family—were accomplished as she was instructed to sell all the oil (verse 7).

How do you feel when God asks you to *pour*—to take that last bit of energy, creativity, or money and spend it just because He said to? Even today, you and I may encounter opportunities and challenges which require more than what we have. And we may be tempted to say, "I have nothing left!" No more strength, no more hope, no more words, no more time.

If that day comes, will you remember the widow's answer "nothing in the house...except" and will you take whatever small thing you do have and *pour,* offer it up to God and allow Him to multiply it into an impossible amount of more?

live these words

Can you think of a time when you felt empty, with nothing left to give? Perhaps it is even today. Do an inventory. What is in your house? List what you do still have, and don't focus on what's missing. For instance, if you are an elderly person who doesn't have the physical or financial ability to invest in certain church projects, you do still have what is needed to be an active participant on the prayer chain.

Ask God to show you how He plans to bring fullness out of what seems to be emptiness in your life. And don't forget to do what is guided, even though it may seem improbable at the time.

pray these words

> *Lord, I am poured out; I come to You for renewal.*
> *Lord. I am weary; I come to You for refreshment.*
> *Lord, I am worn; I come to You for restoration.*
> *Lord, I am lost; I come to You for guidance. Lord,*
> *I am troubled; I come to You for peace. Lord, I*
> *am lonely; I come to You for love. Come Lord,*
> *come revive me. Come reshape me. Come mould*
> *me in Your image. Recast me in the furnace of*
> *Your love. Amen.*

                              ℘ Celtic Prayer[16]

Day 6

...PRAY all the time; thank God no matter
what happens. This is the way God wants
you who belong to Christ Jesus to live.
1 Thessalonians 5:17 THE MESSAGE

I was once privileged to know a man whose life was a
constant prayer—Dr. J. Christy Wilson, Jr., my facul-
ty advisor at Gordon Conwell Theological Seminary. Dr.
Wilson had grown up in Iran and spent most of his life
ministering in Afghanistan until political unrest forced his
family to leave the country a year before I met him in the
late 1970s.

I am indebted to him for teaching me how to "pray
all the time."

Whenever someone mentioned a prayer need, Dr.
Wilson stopped whatever he was doing and said, "Let's just
pray about this right now." And we did! Wherever we were,

whatever was going on, we entered into the presence of God and laid our needs before His throne of grace.

The professor's practice of praying on the spot provided great opportunity for mischief among some seminarians in our missions lecture class. When a fellow student fell asleep, he was nudged awake and told that Dr. Wilson had just called on him to pray. He stood up immediately and led the class in prayer while we all snickered. Our professor simply said, "Thank you very much," as though it were the most natural thing in the world.

Through the years, I've imitated Dr. Wilson by praying immediately for people and situations that are mentioned to me (rather than putting them on a list for later or forgetting altogether.)

This practice certainly caused some anguish among my young children when I'd be driving them around town and praying aloud for this or that. "Don't close your eyes, Mama!" they would frantically holler from the back seat.

In a personal evangelism class I took with Dr. Wilson, we were instructed to pray by name for every student pictured in the student directory—every single day. There were hundreds of seminarians, and our final exam was a print out in which we had to match names and pictures. Now, this test was harder than you might think, unless you had gotten to know them through constant intercessory prayer.

To this day I use a similar strategy when I pray through the lists of attendees at an upcoming conference, students in a class, or most recently, all the guests at our family weddings.

In fact, at the rehearsal dinner when I finally met some New Orleans friends of the groom who had come to our daughter's wedding, it was easy to call them by name.

When they seemed shocked at my familiarity, I let it slip that I'd been praying for them for months.

But seriously. How can we possibly "pray all the time?"

Brother Lawrence—famed for his beloved classic *The Practice of the Presence of God*—reminds us that constant prayer is accomplished by recognizing God with us in every moment. "We can't escape life's dangers without the actual and continual help of God. We need to pray all the time. And how can we pray to Him without being with Him? How can we be with Him unless we think of Him often? And how can we often think of Him unless by a holy habit of thought?"[17]

Brother Lawrence calls this having holy habits. I agree that the more I keep my mind and heart focused on God, the more prayer and thanksgiving spontaneously erupt from my mouth.

Others encourage us to pray even as we breathe. Breathe prayers, in and out, rehearsing God's love and provision, confessing our need for mercy.

> Breathe in: *Lord, I receive what You give.*
> Breathe out: *Lord, I give thanks for what you give.*

I'm quite often shooting up what I call arrow prayers —spontaneous pleadings for guidance or protection or gratitude. Contemporary author Anne Lamott freely admits that her two favorite prayers are "Help, help, help" and "Thanks, thanks, thanks."

Sounds good to me.

Sometimes after a long conversation with friends or an extensive planning meeting, I will wrap up the time with a prayer committing all we've covered to the Lord. I can offer up all our discussions as prayer points because God has heard us already. He knows our concerns. He knows we need an answer for this puzzling predicament. But in making our words a prayer, we acknowledge that we are actually bringing ourselves to the only One who can help.

Francis de Sales urged us to "present our souls to God a thousand times a day. Sprinkle in a season of short prayers on your daily living. If you see something beautiful, thank God for it. If you are aware of someone's need, ask God to help. You can toss up many such prayers all day long. They will help you in your meditation and in your secular employment as well. Make a habit of it."[18]

Perhaps my favorite part of today's verse is where we are urged to "Thank God no matter what happens." While it's impossible to thank God for everything that happens, we can certainly learn the habit of thanking Him in all circumstances.

May we receive with open hands all God allows to come our way.

Know that it is also with those same open hands that we lift up and offer back to Him who we are and how we will respond to such gifts. "Thank you, Lord" should be the prayer that is on our lips at all times in all circumstances.

Prayer is truly a habit that can be developed by even the feeblest of Christ-followers over time. And think of the joy and strength we receive in the process.

live these words

How can you grow in your own prayer life? I encourage you to try one practical suggestion made in this chapter and see how it works for you. I believe in constant and extemporaneous prayer. But I also believe in more substantial prayer times when we are focused on covering all aspects of confession, intercession, petition, and thanksgiving to the God who hears. I often pray John Stott's simple Morning Prayer, always including the Lord's prayer.

Try praying everywhere about everything and don't forget to breathe.

Breathe in: *Lord, I receive what You give.*
Breathe out: *Lord, I give thanks for what You give.*

pray these words

Good morning heavenly Father, good morning Lord Jesus, good morning Holy Spirit. Heavenly Father, I worship You as the Creator and Sustainer of the universe. Lord Jesus, I worship You, Savior and Lord of the world. Holy Spirit, I worship You, Sanctifier of the people of God. Glory to the Father, and to the Son, and to the Holy Spirit. Heavenly Father, I pray that I may live this day in Your presence and please You more and more. Lord Jesus, I pray that this day I may take up my cross and follow You. Holy Spirit, I pray that this day You will fill me with Yourself and cause Your fruit to ripen in my life: love, joy, peace, patience, kindness, goodness, faithfulness, gentleness and self-control. Holy, blessed and glorious Trinity, three persons in one God, have mercy upon me. Amen.

☙ John R. W. Stott (1921-2011)[19]

Day 7

wash

...*WASH* yourself seven times in the Jordan,
and your flesh will be restored and you
will be cleansed. 2 Kings 5:10

*D*o you want to be healed?" Jesus once asked a man who had been waiting thirty-seven years by the healing waters of the pool of Bethesda.

Seems like a no-brainer, yet that is the question we are all confronted with, isn't it? In our own pain, our addiction, our sorrow will we really do anything in order to be healed? Do we want it badly enough?

&

He was handsome, rich, and highly respected. But he was sick with a dreadful disease—leprosy. More than anything this general in the Syrian army, Naaman, wanted to be healed. You would think he'd be willing to do anything toward that end, wouldn't you?

It turns out Naaman was like a lot of us, though, desperately wanting what God can give us, but only on our own terms.

His wife's maidservant was a young girl captured from Israel who actually had the temerity to speak up one day and tell her mistress, "...If only my master would see the prophet who is in Samaria! He would cure him of his leprosy" (2 Kings 5:3). Astonishing though it may seem, at this point Naaman was desperate enough to try anything, so he listened to this slave and immediately went to his own king for a letter of introduction to carry with him to the king of Israel.

Who knows what he was thinking. Well, he definitely intended to arrive with an impressive show because we are told that he packed ten changes of clothes, ten talents of silver, and six thousand shekels of gold. Unfortunately, when the king of Israel received him and read the letter of intent for healing, he misunderstood and was distraught because he could not possibly heal this powerful man from a neighboring country.

"Why does this fellow send someone to me to be cured of his leprosy? See how he is trying to pick a quarrel with me!" (verse 7).

The servant girl had clearly stated that the prophet would be the healer, not the king. And yet, of course, power seeks power, and so Naaman had gone to where he thought the power lay, only to be turned aside.

At this point Naaman was literally left holding the bag—his money was of no use in his pursuit of wholeness. Yet as hopelessness began to take over, Naaman finally received word that the true healer, Elisha the prophet, was willing to see him. Even though his first attempt was thwarted, he still chose to appear in a show of force with all his horses and chariots. Can't you just see him and his entourage standing outside waiting for the prophet to come forth and prophesy?

Instead, a servant ran out with the message from Elisha, "Go, wash yourself seven times in the Jordan, and your flesh will be restored and you will be cleansed" (verse 10).

This made the Syrian furious. He was expecting something profound, at the very least the prophet himself coming out and standing in authority to call on the name of the Lord for healing. Naaman wanted a big splash, but God had other plans for him—splashing in the river.

Yet even the Jordan River infuriated this man who looked with disdain and said, "Are not...the rivers of Damascus, better than all the waters of Israel? Couldn't I wash in them and be cleansed?" (verse 12).

We are told that he went away in a rage.

Angry that healing had not come in the way he expected. Humiliated that others were not doing his bidding. Too prideful to do a simple, humble task—even if it meant healing.

When I read this story, I am struck to the core at how often I behave like Naaman, especially when I need change or healing. "Lord, deliver me from having a critical spirit and a sharp tongue," I'll pray.

In truth, I may expect a divine-intervention-word-from-heaven-zap-on-the-head answer, with the instant result of my emerging as a sweet lady who never raises her voice. God's plan for my transformation may be more practical than that—learning to hold my tongue, talk less, pray often, choose to praise instead of criticize. Think of the relationship results that would garner if I did learn. And yet think of how long I (and perhaps some of you, too) sit around waiting for the spectacular cure.

Naaman's intuitive and courageous servants challenged him by saying, "...if the prophet had told you to do some great thing, would you not have done it? How much more, then, when he tells you, 'Wash and be cleansed'!" (verse 13). In other words, if you are willing to do something dramatic, why not be willing to do something ordinary?

This paradigm takes the greatness off us and keeps it on God, the great Healer. Our part is to do what He says. Eventually, Naaman complied, "...he went down and dipped himself in the Jordan seven times, as the man of God had told him, and his flesh was restored and became clean like that of a young boy" (verse 14). Finally!

Our story ends with an expression of gratitude to the God of Israel as the now healed man proclaims, "Now I know that there is no God in all the world except in Israel" (verse 15).

What a process it took to get him to a place of recognizing Who held true power and Who alone could restore his life and health. Will you and I listen to instructions and follow them, regardless of whether or not they were what we expected? If we do, we may walk also forward, fresh, clean, and healed.

live these words

Our verb today—*wash*—is an ordinary act that most of us do daily. And yet God so often brings about change or healing through our obedience to His surprising commands. As we follow through on the ordinary, He brings extraordinary healing.

But we must take steps, just as Naaman did in his story.

1. We must recognize that there is something wrong that needs fixing. No matter what wonderful things we have going for us, there is often also a great sickness.

2. We must be open to receiving advice and direction from unexpected sources (though we need to be discerning and wise in what we heed).

3. We must begin a journey in the direction of the help. That route may be a spiritual journey toward the God of all healing. Or it may mean beginning a medical or emotional path through professional help.

4. We must do whatever will bring healing and recovery, without debating the merits of the treatment. If indeed God is the One directing us, we must trust Him.

As we begin to change and become all that He intended for us, we simply must thank Him and proclaim that He alone is worthy.

Which step can you take today? Know that God is with you all the way.

pray these words

To Your cross, O Lord, we come for healing, for You alone can make us whole. We come with the broken-hearted and broken-spirited, for You alone can make us whole. We come with those with broken relationships, for You alone can make us whole. We come with the broken in body or in mind, for You alone can make us whole. We come with the weak and the handicapped, for You alone can make us whole. We come with the sinners and the guilty, for You alone can make us whole. Amen.

                                             ℬ David Adam[20]

day 8

go

GO from your country, your people and your father's household to the land I will show you. Genesis 12:1

*D*id you know that a person can attend Sunday morning church services in North Carolina, then fly all the way across the country to California, arriving just in time to attend the Sunday evening church service? I know this because on the first day of 1981, I did it.

I moved from Montreat, North Carolina, to Menlo Park, California, to start a new job.

As I walked into the church that was to be my place of employment, the preacher was reading these words aloud to the congregation. "The Lord said to Abram, 'Go from your country, your people and your father's household to the land I will show you'" (Genesis 12:1).

In my memory, it was a very dramatic moment.

First, I was entering the back door of a beautiful, large terracotta sanctuary with one very long aisle in front of me. Second, the booming voice of the preacher just happened to belong to Dr. Robert Munger, one of my spiritual heroes and author of the little book *My Heart, Christ's Home,* which had been instrumental in my own spiritual growth.

I'm quite sure my heart fluttered and my mind wondered, "What in the world have I gotten myself into now?" Sitting in the pew, my thoughts strayed to the family and friends I had left behind as I identified with Abram. I was there on a wing and a prayer.

God confirmed to me that the move was indeed His call; my obedient response had brought me to this new chapter in my life.

I needed that confirmation because honestly, I was both scared and excited. Scared because I had no idea how I was going to be Menlo Park Presbyterian Church's first mission pastor, and excited that I could actually pioneer a ministry of my heart on a church staff of like-minded dedicated professionals. Scared because we were in Silicon Valley in the early 1980s and I didn't know the first thing about computers, and excited because I was still in my twenties and ready to learn so much about myself, life, and ministry. Scared because at the time I knew no one west of the Mississippi River, and excited because there were so many new people to meet.

God's call to *go* will often be accompanied by fear and inner turbulence. It may come with joy and excitement, but anxiety is rarely far behind. Companions on our journey often include insecurity, loneliness, and fear of failure.

But isn't the call of Abraham the call for all of us, to leave our safe places and venture forth into the unknown?

God's call included God's covenant promise, "I will make you into a great nation, and I will bless you; I will make your name great, and you will be a blessing. I will bless those who bless you, and whoever curses you I will curse; and all peoples on earth will be blessed through you" (Genesis 12:2-3).

The very next verse gives Abraham's response (not what he said, but what he *did*). "So Abram went, as the Lord had told him..." (Genesis 12:4).

When God says *go* what is often our first response? *"Where?" "Wait a minute, I'm not finished here yet." "You've gotta be kidding!"* We need more information. We need guidance. We need assurance.

But sometimes we need to just *do it*.

In her book *God's Guidance*, Elisabeth Elliot emphasizes how God most often calls us out in the midst of our ordinary lives. "David was taking care of sheep, the boy Samuel was serving in the temple, and Matthew was collecting taxes when the Lord called them. 'Do the next thing' is one of the best pieces of advice I have ever had. It works in any kind of situation and is especially helpful when we don't know what to do. What if we don't know what the 'next thing' is? We can find something. Some duty lies on our doorstep. The rule is do it. The doing of that thing may open our eyes to the next."[21]

Abraham's long journey began by taking a risk for a promise.

It was a long journey with its fair share of detours, potholes, and meanderings. But he said yes and went. God kept His covenant, too.

And the world was changed forever.

Sure, I took a risk too, when I moved 3,000 miles from home and began a trajectory toward a life I'd never imagined but an adventure that continues to unfold in amazing ways. I went because of God's call and His covenant. And because I believed then, as I do now, the words of this anonymous poem.

The will of God will never take you,
Where the grace of God cannot keep you,
Where the arms of God cannot support you,
Where the riches of God cannot supply your needs,
Where the power of God cannot endow you.

The will of God will never take you,
Where the love of God cannot enfold you,
Where the mercies of God cannot sustain you,
Where the peace of God cannot calm your fears,
Where the authority of God cannot overrule for you.[22]

live these words

Where has God asked you to go lately? To church? Next door to new neighbors? On a short-term mission trip? To the gym? To that recovery group? To the adoption agency? To school? To the doctor? To visit your estranged brother? Remember that God's call doesn't always include a 3,000-mile move or a long journey. Sometimes we only need to take a few steps in response to discover His will in something new.

Where will you *go* this week? In obedience to His call, what new step will you take?

pray these words

My Lord God, I have no idea where I am going. I do not see the road ahead of me. I cannot know for certain where it will end. Nor do I really know myself, and the fact that I think I am following Your will does not mean that I am actually doing so. But I believe that the desire to please You does in fact please You. And I hope I have that desire in all that I am doing. I hope that I will never do anything apart from that desire. And I know that if I do this, You will lead me by the right road though I may know nothing about it. Therefore, I will trust You always though I may seem to be lost and in the shadow of death. I will not fear, for You are ever with me, and You will never leave me to face my perils alone. Amen.

                                  ʂ Thomas Merton (1915-1968)[23]

day 9

CALL to Me and I will answer you and tell you great and unsearchable things you do not know. Jeremiah 33:3

*W*hat is it like to be available 24/7?

Just ask a teenager. They know.

Recent statistics say that 4 out of 5 teens actually sleep next to their cell phones (and not just for the alarm feature).

Why?

To be instantly available to their peers.

But when self-esteem hinges on peer acceptance, it's a difficult obligation to always be available, whether you want to or not. One psychologist found that "many teens report stories of friends getting insulted, angry, or upset if a text message or phone call is not responded to immediately. 'People will wake me up in the middle of the night and I have to wake up and talk or they will think I'm mad at them or something.'

"Unfortunately, there are hidden dangers of constant digital connection, not the least of which is lack of sleep and sufficient down time unplugged. Experts agree that we have provided our teens with a high-tech world of endless connectivity. "Now we must also insure for them the ingredients of privacy, balance, space, and time to make it safe as well as vital."[24]

It's simply unhealthy for people of any age to be constantly on call. What if those same teens (and their parents) knew that there is One who is available 24/7 whenever He is called upon, without any technology involved at all?

That would be God.

In fact, folks who make up cute sayings have coined the phrase "God's telephone number—Jeremiah 333."

Our word today insists that we do something—*call* on God. He is "sitting by the phone" waiting for us to reach out with our need, our request, our questions, our thanks, our love.

Best of all, He promises He will *always* answer.

No busy signal. No automatic voicemail. No airplane mode or forwarding message. He will answer in ways we cannot even fathom.

But first, we have to *call*.

ശശശശ

Bart was a bit shy because he was different. Well, to be frank, his difference was that he was handicapped. So people often passed him by or ignored him altogether. They wished that he and his problem would simply disappear, but he figured it was just as much his right to frequent that busy road as anyone else. He begged others to help him. In fact, he had been doing just that for as long as he could remember.

To no avail.

No one heard him. No one stopped.

Until that celebrity came to town.

The guy everyone was talking about appeared with his entourage of followers, loudly discussing important issues of the day. Never had Bart heard such a ruckus and never had he wanted more to *be* heard.

His *call* came from deep within, desire and desperation overcoming his shyness and fear of upsetting the status quo, "Jesus, Son of David, have mercy on me!"

Jesus heard.

In the midst of life's cacophony, that anguishing, desperate cry was hard to miss. The crowd was embarrassed for the young master to see such an imperfect resident of their fair town, but they could no longer silence Bartimaeus, nor could they stop the blind beggar from tossing his robe aside and stumbling toward the man.

"What do you want me to do for you?" Jesus asked the one who had so bravely called upon him.

What a question! How would you and I respond to that? The King of the universe answers our call by asking what *we* want Him to do for *us*.

The sky's the limit. He owns it all, anyway.

So this is definitely not a time to settle for small favors, this is time for a bold request, full of desire and faith.

"Rabbi, I want to see."

In other words, "I don't just want something that anyone could provide, like a ride home or a free lunch or even a job. I want a miracle, and I believe You can come through for me on this one."

And he was right. Jesus answered the call with *great and unsearchable things.*

"Go," said Jesus, "your faith has healed you."

Immediately Bartimaeus received his sight.

This story, found in Mark 10:46-52, ends with, "He followed Jesus along the road."

Bart was never the same again. His whole life's identity had been dictated by his blindness, but now that he could see, it was time to move on down a different path.

With Jesus.

Friends, we don't have to sleep with our cell phones in order to maintain constant contact with a dear Friend. The One who will always answer when we call.

Bart would probably love to tell you all about Him.

live these words

Bartimaeus had a deep desire to be healed—to see. Surely Jesus knew this, and yet He still asked the question, "What do you want me to do for you?" Could that be because it is in the recognizing of our deepest desire and calling it out to God that we take the first step toward discovering *great and unsearchable things?* Take some time to prayerfully determine how you would answer that question. As you do, reflect on these words from *Sacred Rhythms*:

"Your desire for more of God than you have right now, your longing for love, your need for deeper levels of spiritual transformation than you have experienced so far is the truest thing about you. You might think that your woundedness or your sinfulness is the truest thing about you or that your giftedness or your personality type or your job title or your identity as husband or wife, mother or father, somehow defines you. But in reality, it is your desire for God and your capacity to reach for more of God than you have right now that is the deepest essence of who you are. There is a place within each one of us that is spiritual in nature, the place where God's Spirit witnesses with our spirit about our truest identity. From this place we *cry out to God* for deeper union with Him and with others."[25]

After you have determined your answer to the same question Jesus posed to Bartimaeus, *call* out to Him, expecting an answer. Then, in grace, take one step forward to act on what He reveals to you.

pray these words

To you, O LORD, I call; my Rock, be not deaf to me, lest, if You be silent to me, I become like those who go down to the pit. Hear the voice of my pleas for mercy, when I cry to You for help, when I lift up my hands toward Your most holy sanctuary. Do not drag me off with the wicked, with the workers of evil, who speak peace with their neighbors while evil is in their hearts. Give to them according to their work and according to the evil of their deeds; give to them according to the work of their hands; render them their due reward. Because they do not regard the works of

the Lord or the work of His hands, He will tear
them down and build them up no more.

Blessed be the Lord! For He has heard the voice
of my pleas for mercy. The Lord is my strength
and my shield; in Him my heart trusts, and I am
helped; my heart exults, and with my song I give
thanks to Him. The Lord is the strength of His
people; He is the saving refuge of His anointed.
Oh, save Your people and bless Your heritage! Be
their Shepherd and carry them forever. Amen.

      ⁖ King David in Psalm 28 (ESV)

day 10

WAIT for the Lord; be strong, and let your heart take courage; wait for the Lord! Psalm 27:14

*A*t twenty-eight I was tired of waiting.

For a husband.

I had tried to be patient. Rather than moping around, I had spent my post university years pursuing life to the fullest—graduate school, a variety of challenging jobs, fascinating people, and international travel.

But with no prospects in sight, I finally concluded that God needed some specific help.

I decided to go away and spend a day in prayer on the matter.

I've been taught to pray boldly, to dream big, yet to always confirm "Thy will be done." Rather than actually telling God how to answer my prayers, I shared my desire and vision, leaving it up to Him how and when to answer.

At least, this is what I do in theory. In practice, sometimes I try to coach Him.

I returned home from my prayer day with a long list typed on my Daytimer notebook paper. A list of twenty-four characteristics that I was praying for in a husband. I still have it. The paper is quite worn because I prayed daily through that list for at least three more years.

- Strong commitment to the Lord; good theology; able to verbalize and share faith

- Has a vision for reaching the unreached

- From a Christian family

- World Christian—open to missions and has traveled abroad

- Strong spiritual leader and would easily take that role in our marriage and family

- Would see my spiritual strength, gifts, and commitment as positive, not as threat

- Wants children and willing to spend significant time as a father raising them

- Committed to trying to live as simply as we can

- Knows how to budget money and handle financial affairs

- Believes in having an open home and extending hospitality to others

- Honest and open—a good communicator

- Believes in this priority system:
  1) God, 2) Family, 3) Ministry/vocation

- Loves me just the way I am but wants to help and encourage me to become the woman God made me to be

- Communicates openly to me—able to be vulnerable

- Strong, yet gentle

- Thinks I'm beautiful (I suppose this also means he needs glasses)

- Intelligent (at least college graduate)

- Doesn't care if I'm not super athletic; likes me to be feminine

- Feels comfortable with my family

- Good sense of humor

- Committed to tithing at least 10 percent to the Lord's work

- Knows manners and common courtesies

- Likes to spend time outdoors

- Has never been married before

So I prayed and I prayed. I waited and I waited.

In the meantime, I went around the world (a second time) speaking and ministering. I went to dozens of weddings. I went to work every day and sought to grow as a woman and a Christ-follower. I became a doting aunt to nieces and nephews.

Sometimes I got discouraged and despaired of the wait. But as one of my friends and prayer mentors Jennifer Kennedy Dean points out "When it appears from earth that God is delaying, He is really putting pieces together that you and I had not thought of. He is engineering circumstances so that His power and glory will be on display. When God builds a waiting period into the course of your affairs, it means that what He is doing requires it. His apparent delays are loving, purposeful, and deliberate."[26]

I'm sure this was the case for me.

God knew there were areas I needed to grow in so I would be ready for the unique family responsibilities that would eventually come my way. And, if you are in the "waiting room" for something you desperately desire, be assured that God is orchestrating your life for His own good purposes.

So it was, that one day at my office in the San Francisco area I had an appointment with a man from Seattle. It lasted all morning and when we parted, he asked for my itinerary (because I was leaving the next day for a month of speaking in Africa).

Several weeks later, when I landed in Tunisia, there was a letter waiting with a request for a date. One thing led to another and within a year, we were married.

My fourth child says her favorite thing on my prayer list for a husband is the last one—*has never been married before.*

"Mama, when God saw that, He laughed!"

The person who was the answer to my waiting prayers did embody twenty-three of the twenty-four qualities...except that last one. Mike was a widower with three small children.

I should have known that God had something even better in mind—*four* new people to love instead of just one. After our wedding, I went through the legal adoption process as a sign of commitment to them.

Our verse today implores us to *wait* on the Lord but also to *let your heart take courage*. Then a few chapters later, the psalmist says yet again, "Be strong, and let your heart take courage, all you who wait for the Lord" (Psalm 31:24 NRSV).

It seems that a need for courage goes hand in hand with waiting. Perhaps that is because God knows that in the waiting, we can sometimes give in to fear. Fear that God doesn't know what we are going through. Fear that God will never answer our prayers. Fear that nothing will ever change.

Let us allow Jesus to be our example of someone who was willing to wait. Remember, He waited thirty years before even beginning his public ministry. From our perspective, that timing can be hard to understand. "We wonder what Jesus could have accomplished if he had started earlier and had longer to minister. But Jesus waited. He waited in the wilderness. He waited in the garden. He waited for His own execution. He waited in the tomb. Jesus learned the rhythm of waiting. We must learn the same rhythm if we are to grow, change, and become like Jesus. Although it seems inefficient, waiting is a necessary step toward spiritual maturity. Waiting cannot be bypassed, as much as we might wish that it could. We cannot become like Jesus overnight."[27]

So, take a deep breath. Have courage. Don't waste your wait.

It will be worth it.

live these words

Waiting is never easy. But there are things we can do while waiting so we don't waste important lessons God has for us during the interim. I have found these four exercises helpful:

*W*rite down your prayers and concerns for this situation.

*A*ssure God you truly desire His will in His way.

*I*ntercede in prayer for others you know who are also waiting.

*T*ake the next step that has been made clear to you.

"God is for you. I can't promise God will always give you the answer you want. I can't promise that He will answer on your timeline. But I can promise this: He answers every prayer, and He keeps every promise. That is Who He is. That is what He does. And if you have the faith to dream big, pray hard, and think long, there is nothing God loves more than proving His faithfulness."[28]

pray these words

God, where are You? What have I done to make You hide from me? Are you playing cat and mouse with me, or are Your purposes larger than my perceptions? I feel alone, lost, forsaken. You are the God who majors in revealing Yourself. You showed Yourself to Abraham, Isaac and Jacob. When Moses wanted to know what You looked like, You obliged him. Why them and not me? I am tired of praying. I am tired of asking.

I am tired of waiting. But I will keep on praying and asking and waiting because I have nowhere else to go. Jesus, You, too, knew the loneliness of the desert and the isolations of the cross. And it is through Your forsaken prayer that I speak these words. Amen.

ა Richard Foster[29]

day 11

praise

PRAISE the Lord, my soul, and never forget
all the good He has done. Psalm 103:2 GW

Ann woke up every day wishing she was dead. So she
wouldn't have yet another opportunity to wreck everything.

As a Canadian farmer's wife and mother of six
homeschooled children, she still carried scars from
childhood tragedy and was unable to truly embrace the
life-changing grace she knew God freely offered.

Until that day she took a friend up on a dare—to
try to write a list of a thousand things she loved, gifts she
already had.

"Before I knew it, thankfulness to God began to fully
change me. Through this intentional daily practice of giving

thanks, I found myself on a transformation journey that affected every aspect of my life—including all the broken places. God began to show me the graces, the love gifts that were right before me, waiting to be noticed, waiting to be received. What I actually found was more daily wonder and surprising beauty than I ever expected. And in a few short years, this daily hunt for God's grace, His glory, had ushered me into a fuller life. A life of joy!"[30]

As Ann Voskamp began recognizing and recording in a blog all she had been given, her transformed life began to spur others to live these words as well. "I stayed up late for too long and wrote a book—*One Thousand Gifts*—and God put it on the *New York Times* Bestseller List for something like 59 weeks so far. It's proof that God really does use broken, messed up, and fallible lives anyway...." Ann says by way of introduction on her popular blog AHolyExperience.com.

What happens when we make a deliberate choice to *praise the Lord* and *never forget all the good He has done?*

We become people whose lives overflow at every point from gratitude.

Back around the time my New England church was gathered (1635), George Herbert captured beautifully what it means to live a life of constant praise.

> "Thou that hast given so much to me,
>
> Give one thing more, a grateful heart...
>
> Not thankful when it pleaseth me;
>
> As if Thy blessings had spare days:
>
> But such a heart whose pulse may be
>
> Thy praise."[31]

Is your heartbeat—your pulse—a constant sound of "Thank you, Lord, for this. Thank you, Lord, for that."

"Well," you say, "sometimes I don't feel thankful or I don't have much to thank God for in the middle of confusion."

True praise is unconditional. It is a choice to thank God anyway however He chooses to resolve difficulties. We can always thank Him for His presence in the midst of each situation. When we praise, we enthrone God in our lives and circumstances. As we recognize His kingship, He stoops to join us and walk us through.

Our praise releases His power. "We become filled to overflowing with Him. Our lives become a stage on which He, the leading Actor, reveals Himself in love and power, blessing both us and the people we relate to."

It is no accident that today I discovered 365 different admonitions in the Bible to *praise*—one for every single day of the year. What if each of those days was filled with our own words of gratitude, praise, and thanksgiving? Do you suppose our lives would be transformed as radically as Ann's?

Absolutely.

Now keep in mind, this kind of praise is not just a Pollyanna "glad game" or optimistic outlook. We are not negating the fact that while there is so much happening that is praiseworthy (and indeed we need to be searching daily for such opportunities), there is also pain and suffering all around us. Our praise does not ignore the struggles but chooses to thank God for His presence in the middle of them, for His power to help us live as overcomers, and for His purposes that will be revealed as a result of our perseverance.

"To thank God in all is to give God glory in all. Is this not our chief end? Murmuring thanks doesn't deny that an event is a tragedy and neither does it deny that there's a cracking fissure straight across the heart. Giving thanks is only this: making the canyon of pain into a megaphone to proclaim the ultimate goodness of God. Our thanks to God is our witness to the goodness of God when Satan and all the world would sneer at us to recant."[32]

It's hard to praise when you've been faithful to God and still find yourself beaten and shackled in a dank, dark prison. Just ask Paul and Silas. They've been there. And yet...

In the middle of their desperate situation, they choose to live the words—to *praise*. By midnight, other prisoners cannot believe what they are hearing in the dungeon. That praise transforms the situation—an earthquake breaks the whole prison wide open, providing escape and freedom (Acts 16:25-26).

Praise is warfare. Our praises are a powerful force against the enemy. When we *praise* God, He tears down the walls of whatever prison has built up around our own souls.

He sets us free.

God inhabits the praises of His people. (See Psalm 22:3.) He dwells within us, even as the words of gratitude flow from our lips.

Start counting.

live these words

I have been keeping thankful lists since I was a little girl and my parents required it as my ticket to Thanksgiving dinner. Recently I discovered my list from

1965, in which I praised God for seventy different things, all neatly categorized. In addition to spontaneous gratitude, for the past several years, my husband and I have enjoyed the discipline of writing down one specific praise item each day. For this purpose, every December I go to the dollar store and buy two of those small datebooks with about an inch of space per day. They are small enough to keep in your briefcase or purse, and by the end of the year you have a wonderful record of daily God-sightings.

If you are brave enough to take on the dare of daily writing down gifts you have been given, be prepared. Your life will change.

pray these words

> *We are only a fraction of Your enormous creation, Lord, but we still want to praise You. You have made us for Yourself and our hearts are restless until they rest in you...The faith You infused in me, Lord, cries out to You. O God, You are the greatest and the best, the strongest, the most merciful and just, absolutely concealed and absolutely present, beautiful, mysterious, never changing, but changing everything, never new, yet never old, always in action, yet always at rest, attracting all things to Yourself but needing none, preserving and fulfilling and sheltering, conceiving and nourishing and ripening, continually seeking but lacking nothing, You love without the confusion of emotion, You are jealous, but without fear. You owe us nothing and yet You give to us as though You were indebted to us. You forgive what is due You, and*

yet lose nothing Yourself. After all of this, what have I said? What can anyone say when speaking of God? Amen.

ဟ Augustine Confessions A.D. 354-430[33]

day 12

live

...**LIVE** a life worthy of the Lord and please Him in every way: bearing fruit in every good work, growing in the knowledge of God.... Colossians 1:10

> The truth is out. We *will* all die.
> The question is, will we all *live*?

I looked at the water-stained journal from 1949, smudged not only by years, but by miles. Sighing deeply and close to tears, I carefully typed the words on the blank white paper... "Wherever you are, be all there. Live to the hilt every situation you believe to be the will of God."

In my early twenties at the time, I couldn't help but think of the young man who had penned these words—Jim

Elliot, missionary to Ecuador who was speared to death in 1956 by the very Indians he had sought to help. Truly here was a man who knew how to embrace life fully.

And I, a seminary student, was helping his widow, author Elisabeth Elliot, type her newest book manuscript, which was published as *The Journals of Jim Elliot*.

Many years have passed since I first read those words, but I vividly remember asking God back then to help me *'live to the hilt'* all the days He would give me. And today I realize that in my actual day-by-day living I have learned so very much about God's constant presence, unconditional love, steadfast faithfulness, redeeming grace, and undeserved mercy.

It is true, as Annie Dillard reminds us, that "how we spend our days is, of course, how we spend our lives."

The sad reality is that many of us spend our days just coasting through life as though we had time to waste.

As I write today, I know five different friends (all across this country) who have been told they have an illness from which they will most certainly die. They are all near my own age and have spent their lives in various forms of ministry. The only difference between us is that I have not been *told* I have only a short time to live.

How would receiving that kind of prognosis affect our response to God's word to *live*? I would hope it would make us embrace each day as a gift and savor the moments, rather than just going through the motions.

In Thornton Wilder's play "Our Town," Emily, who has died, has the opportunity to visit her life for one day. As she observes everyone just going through the motions, she recognizes life for the treasure that it was. "Let's really look at one another! I can't go on. It goes so fast. We don't have time to look at one another. I didn't realize. All that was going on in life and we never noticed... Do any human beings ever realize life while they live it—every, every minute?"[34]

Do you spend your days embracing life?

Jesus announced, "I came so that everyone would have life, and have it in its fullest" (John 10:10 CEV).

Perhaps the greatest gift we could offer back to our Lord is a life well-lived, where moments are not wasted, but savored. A life where we know how important it is to treasure relationships, extend kindness, and act with courage.

Wouldn't that be a life that is *worthy of the Lord* and *pleasing to Him in every way?*

When all is said and done, life will be reduced to a few words, hopefully not like these written about an evil king who did wrong in the eyes of the Lord. "Jehoram was thirty-two years old when he became king, and he reigned in Jerusalem eight years. He passed away, to no one's regret, and was buried in the City of David, but not in the tombs of the kings" (2 Chronicles 21:20).

It's sobering to think of the essence of a life in such limited words.

A few years ago someone discovered a six-word story by Ernest Hemingway: "For sale: Baby shoes, never worn." A magazine editor then got the idea to run a "Six-Word Memoir" contest that is still ongoing.[35]

The challenge? "Describe your life in six words."

Can you do it?

Not only is it important to *live* our lives, but to embrace the unique story unfolding to the world. "At any age, if we are to face life with integrity and purpose, we must know that our lives do mean something, that we matter to someone, and that whatever story we have lived, it has brought us to this point.... As we touch the stories of Christ and connect them with our stories, we find wholeness."[36]

I was surprised to learn how many people have taken this challenge to write their life story in six words.

As I researched, I found a few favorites. Some have a bright outlook: *"I have time to fix this,"* or *"Still fit into high school earrings."* Others are sad: *"He died before I could apologize,"* or *"Tend to jump on sinking ships."* Some are reflective: *"Like old china; chipped, but cherished,"* or *"Fat. Thin. Fat. Thin. Fat. Thin."* Others are clearly moving forward: *"I refused to be a victim,"* or *"Survived the divorce. Learned to live."*

While trying to come up with my own six-word life story I asked myself several questions.

- ❧ What was a particular struggle or challenge in my life?
- ❧ What precipitated the most positive change in me?
- ❧ Where do I hope the rest of my life will be focused?

Of course, I had hundreds of answers to all these questions. Literally. But, for the sake of the exercise, I edited down to the basics.

One of my particular struggles in life was always striving to *be* more, *do* more, *achieve* more...thinking God would then love me more. That's bad theology and an even worse lifestyle.

What changed me the most was learning about God's amazing *grace*—the life-giving gift we don't deserve and can never earn. He already loves and accepts me based on who He is, not what I do. This realization led me to the way I seek to live out the rest of my life—in *daily gratitude* for all God's many blessings.

The end product—my six words: "Tried hard. Embraced grace. Forever thankful."

What words will you *live* today?

live these words

Life can be over in a second. Just ask my friend Paula, whose teenage son encountered ice on the road midday and was instantly killed in a car crash. We all know life is fragile, but we must not forget that life is also a precious gift to be savored every moment. Mitch Albom, a young journalist, made this discovery when he began visiting his old professor who was dying from ALS. In *Tuesdays with Morrie,* he observes, "So many people walk around with a meaningless life. They seem half asleep, even when they're busy doing things they think are important. This is because they're chasing the wrong things." [37]

Are you chasing the wrong things? What are you investing in that will last? God has given each of us more than we can possibly imagine, "...no eye has seen, no ear has heard, and no mind has imagined what God has prepared for those who love him" (1 Corinthians 2:9 NLT).

The question is, what will you do with what you've been given? Just before he died, a young man named Randy gave *The Last Lecture.* Perhaps it would be helpful to heed his words. "We have a finite amount of time. Whether short or long, it doesn't matter. Life is to be lived!"[38]

Where have you been wasting precious time? Stop.

pray these words

Here am I, O God, lifting up heart and voice to Thee. ... Dear Father, take this day's life into Thine own keeping. Control all my thoughts and feelings. Direct all my energies. Instruct my mind. Sustain my will. Take my hands and make them skillful to serve Thee. Take my feet and make them swift to do Thy bidding. Take my eyes and keep them fixed upon Thine everlasting beauty. Take my mouth and make it eloquent in testimony to Thy love. Make this a day of obedience, a day of spiritual joy and peace. Make this day's work a little part of the work of the Kingdom of my Lord Jesus Christ, in whose name these my prayers are said. Amen.

                       ℘ John Baillie (1886-1960)[39]

day 13

persevere

...PERSEVERE so that when you have done the will of
God, you will receive what He has promised.
Hebrews 10:36

What does a thirty-four-year-old man do when he hears
these two phrases only days apart. "Congratulations,
you have a baby daughter!" and "I'm so sorry to tell you
that your wife has liver cancer?"

I'll tell you what he does. He makes a choice to move
forward into each new day, trusting in God's strength, and
seeking to fulfill his calling as loving husband and father.

He *perseveres*.

At least that's the way my husband, Michael
McDowell, faced life when he and his first wife, Inka, were
confronted with the unthinkable as a young couple.

This verse in Hebrews calls us to do the will of God, but what if the will of God involves walking through the suffering of someone you love? Holding your family together while juggling work, childcare, medical appointments, and household, all the while watching the love of your life grow weaker, cancer diminishing her vibrant young life?

Perseverance means to keep going, and it's a particularly difficult verb to live out because its very nature means struggle.

"At first the whole thing was surreal," Mike recalls. "I remember standing in the kitchen on the telephone, absolutely stunned and speechless, hearing the doctor's prognosis that was about to turn our lives upside down. Yet, through the amazing help of our family and God's family, we sought treatment and surgery for Inka, cared for the three kids, and felt hopeful that the cancer was completely eradicated.

"By the end of the year we were all devastated when the cancer returned with a vengeance."

One thing that helped Mike keep going was the example of his own parents, who had survived the death of their seven-year-old son Greg, battled financial hardship, and struggled with their own medical challenges. "I learned at an early age to never give up. And my ministry at the time—InterVarsity outreach to college students, which required raising support each month—taught me that God could be trusted to provide, no matter what the circumstances."

Spiritual perseverance gains for each of us a reward from above if we know that the suffering is only part of the process toward a deeper life with God. "...we also glory in our sufferings, because we know that suffering produces perseverance; perseverance, character; and character, hope" (Romans 5:3-4).

As Inka's condition worsened, she wanted to be near her family in the Netherlands, so Mike transferred there and moved everyone into a Dutch flat, never realizing he would be a widower within the month. Still, he stayed in that foreign country, learned the language, and kept his two sons and daughter well cared for an additional two years before returning to the States.

Today, those same kids are the age he was during this ordeal.

He recently shared how he was able to *persevere* through so many hard times. "I cannot imagine going through the life I've lived without a solid sense of God's presence, love, and care for me at all times. There are many ways I experienced this. First of all, through community. The body of Christ, along with our own family, 'held up my arms' like Aaron did for Moses in the Bible."

"When I was too tired or perplexed to handle a situation, I would often find someone else quietly cleaning our home or making special ed. arrangements for our son, or (in a most generous surprise) anonymously providing a final family trip for all of us to Hawaii. I still meet people who remember praying for Inka back in the 1980s. Those prayers sustained us.

"Secondly, I found that in the midst of horrific change, God never changes. One way this sustained me was through my own spiritual disciplines of prayer, worship, the sacraments, and Bible reading. Those are the touchstones not only for my life, but for the lives of countless saints through the ages. There's a reason we commit God's Word to memory in the good times—so that it can be remembered in the bad times, and bring hope.

"And lastly, in order to *persevere*, I simply learned to take the next step.

"We cannot survive on our feelings. Many times I didn't feel like getting up and changing my daughter's diaper or biking the boys to school, but actually those ordinary routines were what kept me going. Yes, it's hard to be a single parent, but knowing those precious lives depend on you is a great boost to focus beyond your own pain," Mike concluded.

In *The Devout Life*, Francis de Sales shows how important it is for each of us to resolve to stay with God that we may *receive what He has promised.* "A compass needle always points north regardless of the ship's course. If we will aspire toward God, the confusing changes of life will not unsteady us. Nothing can separate us from God's love. When little bees are caught in a storm they take hold of small stones so that they can keep their balance when they fly. Our firm resolution to stay with God is like stability to the soul amid the rolling waves of life."[40]

My husband these past thirty years, Michael McDowell, exhibits that "stability of soul" and has modeled that for our four children (and me) his entire life. In these decades since Inka died, there have been other challenges confronting him with the choice to give up or keep on.

He chose to *persevere*. Will you?

live these words

What situation/diagnosis/news stopped you in your tracks recently? What was your very first reaction? Run?

Pray? Scream? Confide in a close friend? But what did you actually *do*? Take some time today and examine your own strategy for choosing to persevere through tough times, using Mike's outline of

1. depending on community;

2. continuing in spiritual disciplines; and

3. taking the next step as your guide.

pray these words

> *O Heavenly Father, I praise and thank You for all Your goodness and faithfulness throughout my life. You have granted me many blessings. Now let me accept tribulations from Your hand. You will not lay on me more than I can bear. You make all things work together for good. For Your children. Amen.*

> Dietrich Bonhoeffer (1906-1945)[41]

day 14

conquer

...*CONQUER* evil by doing good. Romans 12:21 NLT

*W*hat if evil hijacked your youth and held you captive for years and years? When escape to a new life was finally achieved, you would vow to stay as far away from your former captors as possible, right?

Well, maybe not.

Maybe you would choose to return and *conquer evil by doing good.*

Patrick was a sixteen-year-old teenager when he was abducted. There were no milk cartons broadcasting his disappearance, no organizations rescuing young people from human trafficking, no Amber alerts. He was on his own among a fierce pagan people.

He was now a slave, far from home.

In fifth-century Ireland.

The land was lush and beautiful. But the people were themselves enslaved to superstition, spirits, and fear. Violence was common and life was cheap. In this alien land, Patrick grew up quickly as slave to an Irish chieftain.

When there was time to be lonely and homesick among his heathen captors, Patrick found solace in God and converted to Christianity. He drew close to Him through nature, silence, and prayer. One evening he felt God's Spirit prompting him to go to the shore two hundred miles away. There he discovered a boat which he immediately took as God's provision for his escape.

After six long years he was finally free and able to pursue a new life. With a deepened faith, he pursued ordination in the church and continued a vital ministry in Roman Britain. But the land that first captured him now captured his heart.

He longed to return to Ireland. Patrick had become convinced that he was handpicked by God to convert the entire country to Christianity.

Thomas Cahill, author of the bestselling book *How the Irish Saved Civilization*, believes that Patrick exemplified two major characteristics, humility and strength. "Patrick was certain that he had been called by God to do exactly what he did—return to the land of his captivity and convert the Irish natives to Christianity. In this certainty, Patrick finds sufficient strength to overcome every obstacle he encountered in the remaining years of his life."

When Patrick decided to "willingly go back to the barbarians with the gospel," Cahill explains, "he had to figure out how to bring the values of the gospel he loved to such people. These were people who still practiced human sacrifice, who warred with each other constantly and who were renowned as the great slave traders of the day."[42]

Patrick greatly respected nature, but he also wanted the Irish to know that God was the only One worthy of worship. So he used a shamrock to explain the three persons of the Trinity—God the Father, God the Son, and God the Holy Spirit—one stem, but three leaves.

Patrick labored in Ireland for thirty years, and even though some say he singlehandedly converted Ireland, Patrick preferred to put it this way, "I owe it to God's grace that so many people should, through me, become Christians."

How can we be conquerors of evil? How do we battle for the good?

Perhaps we could learn something from the greatest warriors of all time in the Roman Empire. How did they *conquer*? The shields of Roman soldiers were four feet by two and a half feet rectangular, made of several layers of coated wood. As fiery darts hit the shields, they were extinguished. Helmets made of bronze were heavy, but extremely protective.

During the heyday of the Roman Empire, the soldiers carried out daily maneuvers *even in peace time*, so they would be prepared physically and mentally to withstand battle when it came.

Historian Josephus observed, "No confusion breaks their customary formation, no panic paralyzes, no fatigue exhausts them. By their military exercises, the Romans instill into their soldiers fortitude not only of body, but also of soul."

Unfortunately, Rome eventually brought about its own downfall as disciplines became relaxed. Soldiers said the armor was too heavy, so they didn't use their shields and helmets. Since they didn't practice for battle each day, when the fighting actually came, they were weak and unprepared.[43]

Constant discipline in peace time will reap benefits when battles come. Even in the spiritual realm.

Patrick didn't fight the Irish with swords and armor, but, instead, he followed Paul's admonition to "put on the whole armor of God" (Ephesians 6:10-18). He loved the Irish, and they loved him back, perpetuating many legends about his life and ministry. When this Briton, born as Patricius, died at age 75, he was named Patrick, patron saint of Ireland.

And neither Ireland nor Christianity was ever quite the same.

live these words

In our pursuit of conquering evil with good do we sometimes find the armor burdensome? Is carrying a shield of faith too heavy? Are you tempted to compromise at the workplace, socially, or online? Has your sword dulled from disuse? Are you staying in the Word of God and learning it in your heart so you can know what God wants and how to live? As Christ-followers, we have been equipped with what we need to prevail.

Today's prayer is commonly known as St. Patrick's Breastplate, found in the ancient *Book of Armagh*, from the early ninth century, along with Patrick's authentic "Confession." Patrick is said to have written this prayer to strengthen himself with God's protection as he prepared to confront and convert Loegaire, high king of Ireland.

When St. Paul referred to putting on the "armor of God" in his letter to the Ephesians (6:11) to fight sin and evil inclinations, he could have been thinking of prayers just like this one. We may not wear combat gear in our daily lives, but St. Patrick's Breastplate can function as divine armor for protection against spiritual adversity. Where do you need to *conquer* evil by doing good? Ask God and He will reveal to you His battle plans for your own life.

pray these words

(Author's note: Whenever I pray this prayer, I stand and raise my right hand as though holding a sword. Then I proclaim with great conviction, "I arise today....")

I arise today through a mighty strength, the invocation of the Trinity, through a belief in the Threeness, through confession of the Oneness of the Creator of creation.

I arise today through the strength of Christ's birth and His baptism, through the strength of His crucifixion and His burial, through the strength of His resurrection and His ascension, through the strength of His descent for the judgment of doom.

I arise today through the strength of the love of cherubim, in obedience of angels, in service of archangels, in the hope of resurrection to meet with reward, in the prayers of patriarchs, in preachings of the apostles, in faiths of confessors, in innocence of virgins, in deeds of righteous men.

I arise today through the strength of heaven; light of the sun, splendor of fire, speed of lightning, swiftness of the wind, depth of the sea, stability of the earth, firmness of the rock.

I arise today through God's strength to pilot me, God's might to uphold me, God's wisdom to guide me, God's eye to look before me, God's ear to hear me, God's word to speak for me, God's hand to guard me, God's way to lie before me, God's shield to protect me, God's hosts to save me from snares of the devil, from temptations of vices, from everyone who desires me ill, afar and anear, alone or in a multitude.

I summon today All these powers between me and those evils, Against every cruel and merciless power that may oppose my body and soul, Against incantations of false prophets, Against black laws of pagandom, Against false laws of heretics, Against craft of idolatry, Against spells of witches and smiths and wizards, Against every knowledge that corrupts man's body and soul; Christ to shield me today Against poison, Against burning, Against drowning, Against wounding, So that there may come to me an abundance of reward.

Christ with me, Christ before me, Christ behind me, Christ in me, Christ beneath me, Christ above me, Christ on my right, Christ on my left, Christ when I lie down, Christ when I sit down, Christ in the heart of every man who thinks of me, Christ in the mouth of every man who speaks of me, Christ in the eye that sees me, Christ in the ear that hears me.

I arise today through a mighty strength, the invocation of the Trinity, through a belief in the Threeness, through a confession of the Oneness of the Creator of creation. Amen.

                            ฿ Patrick of Ireland (390-461)[44]

day 15

wake up

WAKE UP. Put your face in the sunlight. GOD's bright glory has risen for you. The whole earth is wrapped in darkness, all people sunk in deep darkness, But God rises on you, His sunrise glory breaks over you. Isaiah 60:1-2
THE MESSAGE

*A*ll I wanted to do was sleep.

Actually, all I wanted to do was bury my head under the pillow, silently singing the old country ballad that goes, "Make the world go away...." I had never felt this defeated, this hopeless, this numb. I seemed to have lost myself.

Worst of all, I believed things would never change.

I had tried so hard to keep going and overcome the lethargy that had seized my soul. But the darkness called me deeper and I was succumbing fast. I needed to *wake up* from this nightmare.

I needed a miracle.

It was no consolation that I had unwillingly joined a group of eighteen million adult Americans diagnosed with depression. Who says misery loves company? I hated being a statistic, but I especially hated that my deep faith and walk with God hadn't protected me from this despair.

Why couldn't I just pull myself up by my bootstraps and gain victory?

At the time, several decades ago now, most Christians weren't aware of the combination of physiological, emotional, and spiritual factors contributing to depression. Few believers in public life had admitted to this journey, and there was still a certain stigma attached. Or maybe that was only in my mind. I assure you my mind played a lot of tricks on me back then.

Today, we now realize that deep depression involves more than emotional suffering. It is not simply a state of mind or a negative view of life, but something that affects our physical being as well.

What I did know back then was that the words of Scripture rang true—*people were sunk in deep darkness,* and I was one of those people clinging to the dark while so very desperate for the light. Seventeenth-century British minister William Bridge once confessed, "Ah, Lord, my prayers are dead, my affections dead, and my heart is dead: but Thou art a living God and I bear myself upon Thee."

When we hit bottom, the most important thing to remember is that God is indeed *Jehovah Rapha*, the One who heals.

He is with us in that deep pit. His power and His might and His mercy and His grace are totally available to us. Our job is to turn to Him, to cry out, "I bear myself upon Thee."

He is the only One who can truly wake us up when all we want to do is sleep.

However, as I discovered in my own healing, the process God often uses takes a village of support—medically, psychologically, spiritually, and emotionally.

It took some time for me to *put my face in the sunlight* and move forward with joy and purpose and strength. Body chemistry needed to be balanced and counseling sessions attended. Prayers of confession and of repentance and prayerful cries for mercy, all offered and received in grace.

And I never want to go back there again.

A recent *Leadership Journal* includes words from Texas pastor Tommy Nelson who also awakened on the other side of such darkness. "Christian counseling can deal with the over-scheduling, the worry, the fear, or whatever else might have contributed to one's depression. But often Christians have a bias against doing anything medical. They feel guilty about taking drugs for a problem that was caused by an emotional or spiritual crisis. They need to realize that the medications are not some sort of 'happy pills' but rather necessary tools for bringing one's body chemistry back to normal."

Nelson continues, "On the other hand, medications can clinically treat the physical symptoms but often not deal adequately with the causes. Both are essential. A pastor should also have someone in his congregation who has experienced depression/anxiety so that the one suffering from it can have someone to talk to."[45]

Someone to talk to.

How key it is to know that we are not alone. King David talked to God from his depths, "Be merciful to me, LORD, for I am in distress; my eyes grow weak with sorrow, my soul and body with grief. My life is consumed by anguish and my years by groaning; my strength fails because of my affliction, and my bones grow weak" (Psalm 31:9-10).

But most of us have no idea what David meant when he further lamented, "I am forgotten as though I were dead" (verse 12). Severe depression is often beyond description. And when such deep and painful feelings cannot be explained, they cut to the heart of one's spiritual being.

I'm not exactly sure why this malady has continued for thousands of years. But I know it is a reality in our culture, so we dare not simply sleep it off. The World Health Organization named depression the second most common cause of disability worldwide after cardiovascular disease, and it is expected to become number one in the next ten years.[46]

You, or someone you love, may eventually face this darkness. And on that day when you can only grasp a sliver of light, hold on to it and remember that God is calling you by name. He loves you with an everlasting love, and He will never let go. He is with you in the darkness, but He will bring you out of it as you begin to move toward Him.

Ours is a chaotic and cruel world at times. If you are feeling small, insignificant, and expendable, I want you to know that you matter. You were created by the One who spun the stars into space. You are unique and have an important role in God's kingdom story. But it will be a real story, not all sunshine and roses. Your story will help others when you live it authentically. For it will be a story of grace. Overcoming darkness. Moving into the Light.

Yes, I've spent some time in the darkness, too. But I'm so thankful I *woke up*.

live these words

Perhaps you know someone who might be depressed. If they have been dealing with symptoms such as these for two weeks or more, strongly suggest they consult a doctor.

- Feeling of sadness
- Sleeping too much or having trouble sleeping
- Irritability
- Low energy
- Problems concentrating
- Losing interest in things they used to enjoy
- Feeling worthless
- Loss of appetite or overeating
- Hopelessness
- Physical symptoms
- Thoughts of suicide

There is help available for each of us in times of darkness, whether it is merely a season of being down and discouraged, or whether it is indeed manifested in despair and depression. Others of us recognize that we are simply sleeping our lives away on many levels and we need a boost to *wake up* and live fully in God's light. Begin wherever you are today, and take a small step into a bright new day calling your name.

pray these words

> *Lord, I recognize my spirit is not fully functional, or fully awake in several areas. I ask Your forgiveness for the ways in which I have wounded those around me, Lord. I ask Your forgiveness for being unwilling to live life. God, I ask You to awaken my spirit. Cleanse my spirit and remove the cobwebs. Thank You for not giving up on me. Touch my ears so I can hear You speaking to me. Lord, I choose life. I make a conscious decision to be fully present and I ask You to hold me to that decision and bring to death in me that impulse to flee. I ask that Your resurrection life strengthen and enable me to develop new ways to respond in each of the areas in which I am slumbering. Help me to see Your call to life as a loving call and set a guard over my life so I can respond to that call in a good way. I thank You, Father God, for my life. Amen.*

ꙮ Anonymous Prayer[47]

day 16

show

...*SHOW* mercy and compassion to one another.
Zechariah 7:9

Don't you worry about your daughter traveling and working in such dangerous countries?" another mom asked me recently.

"Of course I'm concerned, but I pray for her constantly," was my well-rehearsed answer. "God loves our kids more than we do, and I know He is with her."

Well-rehearsed or not, my words were true and I believed them. I was also proud that Fiona had chosen a career path in international development and was now helping to make positive changes for women and children in poor, developing countries.

Yes, sometimes that meant traveling to war-torn places like Baghdad and Islamabad. Sometimes it meant AIDS education in places like Rwanda or Uganda.

But to the people who were in pain, poverty, or political persecution, my daughter had responded by *show[ing] mercy and compassion.*

How often had I heard myself tell young moms, "If you teach your children to care about other people, don't be surprised if they grow up and care about other people!"

Caring also means they will probably want to go on a short-term mission trip or join the Peace Corps or give away all their stuff.

William Tyndale once said, "To be merciful is to have compassion, to feel another's sickness, to mourn with those who are in grief, to suffer with someone in trouble, to help in any way we can, and to comfort with loving words."[48]

When we show compassion and mercy, we offer comfort. In the New Testament, the Greek term most often used to convey this is *paraklesis*—which has a double meaning of both encouragement and consolation.

Jesus taught about this active response when he told the parable of the sheep and goats found in Matthew 25. In the final judgment, all peoples will be separated into two groups, much like a shepherd separates the sheep from the goats. On the right will be those who actually did as Christ commanded, "For I was hungry, and you fed me. I was thirsty, and you gave me a drink. I was a stranger, and you invited me into your home. I was naked, and you gave me clothing. I was sick, and you cared for me. I was in prison, and you visited me" (verses 35-36 NLT). And then, to an incredulous people who didn't understand, He clarified by saying, "…I tell you the truth, when you did it to one of the least of these my brothers and sisters, you were doing it to me!" (verse 40 NLT).

On the left, however, would be the ones who did not actively respond. "I tell you the truth, when you refused to help the least of these my brothers and sisters, you were refusing to help me" (verses 45-46 NLT). Judged and sentenced to eternal punishment.

As Christ-followers we are called to follow Christ, to do what He did, and to do it as unto Him. In his book on Benedictine life, Robert Benson observes, "The picture of Christ that is given us in the Gospels is clear. If we are going to be like Him, then we are to stop by the well and offer water to those who are thirsty. We are to wash the feet of those to whom we have been given. We are to cook breakfast on the shoreline for those who have been up all night. We are to stop in the crowd and try to figure out who has brushed up against us. We are to keep our hearts and arms open for the children when they are trying to get our attention. If doing such things in the world requires that we humbly recognize our call to serve others in all humility, then it is a proper trade to make."[49]

As far back as the Old Testament, our path was clearly set out, "…what does the Lord require of you but to do justice, and to love kindness, and to walk humbly with your God?" (Micah 6:8 RSV). Our response is to determine what that will look like today in our own lives and through our own influence. We are God's Plan A for bringing the kingdom of heaven here on earth. And there is no Plan B.

In the sixteenth century, Teresa of Avila put it this way: "Christ has no body now on earth but yours; no hands but yours; no feet but yours. Yours are the eyes through which the compassion of Christ must look out on the world. Yours are the feet with which He is to go about doing good. Yours are the hands with which He is to bless His people."[50]

So let us be Jesus with skin on today as we *show mercy and compassion.*

live these words

Start where you are. You don't have to cross cultures or geographic boundaries. There are people in your own home, your neighborhood, your office, your school, your streets, who need a touch of compassion and mercy. Re-read the final quote above from Teresa of Avila and search how you can be Christ's.

- ∞ Eyes—Be alert. Be conscious. Look and listen for news of unexpected tragedy or need.

- ∞ Feet—Then show up with something helpful (fresh rotisserie chickens are my stand-by). Or just show up with yourself.

- ∞ Hands—Offer to bless in a practical way—run errands, clean the living room, fill up the car, shovel snow—anything tangible to show you care.

Ask God to make you more alert to others' needs every day. One thing my husband does is notice the label where his clothing is made and offer a spontaneous prayer for the people of that country.

Sometimes we *are* called to venture way beyond our comfort zone, into another realm entirely. Just know that

God will provide you with what you need to be His eyes, feet, and hands in those hard places as well.

pray these words

I pray You would give me a heart for those...who, for whatever reason, are not in the mainstream of life. For those who lie crumpled and cast aside. For those who are forgotten and ignored. For those who are in some way blinded to the fullness of life. Help me not to turn a deaf ear when they call out. Help me to stop, regardless of what the crowd may say. Help me to give them my undivided attention. Help me to give myself to them as You did – to show mercy, to do what I can.

Although I may not be able to loose them from their chains or free them from their separate prisons, Help me to visit faithfully so they may know that someone cares; Help me to bring a meal so they may be nourished; Help me to say a kind word so they may be encouraged; Help me to give a gentle touch so they may be comforted. Help me to lend a listening ear so their stories may be heard. Help me whenever, wherever, and however I can to bring light to someone who sits in darkness. Amen.

                                              ✍ Ken Gire[51]

day 17

commit

COMMIT everything you do to the Lord. Trust Him,
and He will help you. Psalm 37:5 NLT

I'm not very impressed and won't be sending this manuscript to any publisher. Honestly, Cindy, no one wants
this book, so you may as well start over on something else,"
my literary agent said during our appointment at the annual booksellers convention.

I was shattered.

Murmuring something, I made a quick exit, seeking
a quiet place where I could fall apart in private. The project
had already been through several revisions and was, at
least in my opinion, both timely and strategic.

However, my agent had been vehement, almost
personal, in her rejection of the proposal. I managed to

make it back to my hotel room, sobbed to my two author roommates, and started packing for my crack-of-dawn flight home the next day.

To say I was discouraged would be an understatement.

When I trudged through the Los Angeles airport at five o'clock the next morning, I was pretty low. I whispered a prayer, *God, once again, I lay all my writing efforts in Your capable hands. Please show me Your way for my next book, whether it be this one or something entirely different. Thy will be done. Amen.*

Arriving at the gate, I saw clusters of other worn-out folk, lugging briefcases and laptop computers. I turned to the woman next to me and greeted her with some pleasantry, discovering she was on her way home to Denver after attending the same convention. After a bit of friendly chat, she mentioned she was an editor at a large publishing house.

So I threw it out there. What did I have to lose?

"I'm just curious, as you leave the booksellers convention, was there one book idea you had hoped to find from an author?" I said in my most timid, yet interested, manner.

"Well, my boss was interested in something that addresses the whole Baby-Boomers-reaching-middle-age idea. We think that might find a good audience," she replied.

Did I hear her correctly? Had she really just said that her one regret on leaving the convention was not being offered something on the very subject of the book proposal now gathering dust in my own briefcase?

"Uh, well, I, uh, as it happens, I have a book proposal in my briefcase on that very subject. Would you be willing to look it over and see if it might fit your needs?" I stammered.

The startled editor graciously took my manuscript. Within the year, my book on turning fifty, *What We've Learned So Far*, was published in time to celebrate my own half-century mark!

From absolute rejection to acceptance in a series of events that could only have been orchestrated by God.

What does it mean to commit everything we do to the Lord?

The verb *commit* means "to entrust or put in charge." It is a simple act of relinquishment. Not that relinquishing or releasing is ever easy, but it can be a simple process of laying hands on a file full of papers and asking God to bring the project together in a way that will honor Him and build the Kingdom. It also involves the harder internal process of being willing to accept a "no" as an answer or being redirected to give up the project altogether.

I pray over my work all the time, even when it's in the incubation stage. As a conference speaker, I will often come up with titles of presentations based on need or inspiration and then pray over those, asking God to give me the Scripture, the teaching, the stories, and the clear direction whether or not to prepare it. And then, of course, to give me opportunity to speak those words to listening ears.

Life is too short to invest in work that doesn't have God's hand all over it.

The more we know Him, the easier it will be to hear His voice and proceed forward or retreat another way. Timothy stood firm in his conviction when he declared, "...I know whom I have believed and I am persuaded that He is able to keep what I have committed to Him until that Day" (2 Timothy 1:12 NKJV).

Author Mark Batterson recalls committing his first book to the Lord. "In typical God fashion, He exceeded my highest expectations.... I don't just write books; I circle them in prayer. To me, writing is praying with a keyboard. I also recruited a team to pray for me while I wrote the book. Then we prayed circles around the people who would buy the book. We specifically prayed that God would get the book into the right hands at the right time.

"On one level, I'm surprised by the way God has used paragraphs within that book to save marriages and prompt decisions and birth visions. On another level, I'm not surprised at all. It's no coincidence when people tell me that God brought the book into their lives at the perfect time. It's providence. To me, a book sold is not a book sold; it's a prayer answered."[52]

I often think back to that very low point in my writing career.

What if I had continued to pout, lick my wounds, and shuffle through the airport that early morning, retreating to a corner seat and ignoring everyone around me? What if I had simply taken my agent's advice and thrown in the towel?

Instead, I chose to prayerfully continue to *commit* everything to God—the One who called me to write in the first place—and know that He would indeed help me. Can I truly surrender all to Him? Am I willing for any of the *works of my hands* to be taken away or given up for His glory? That's the place where He wants me to be. Would I still commit my writing to Him if that book had never been published?

Whatever the result of our efforts, we can trust the One who created and sustains us. Relinquish. Surrender. *Commit.* And then move forward with His help.

live these words

Today's Scripture speaks of committing everything to God—yes, our work, but also our relationships, our health, our finances, our responsibilities, our dreams, our concerns. We are told that if we trust Him, we will be helped. What does commitment look like in your own life? Pick one of those categories that you need to hand over to the Lord.

Take finances, for an example. Why not lay out your bills, your budget, your checkbook, your paystub, anything that might represent this area in which you need God's help. Pray over these symbols, committing them to Him and asking for guidance and clarity over your financial responsibilities. Listen and be prepared to follow His leading. Does that mean the answer will always be money to spare, or, as in my story, a book contract? Absolutely not. Sometimes we will see amazing answers and other times we will be asked to wait, or choose another path. Yet all may be considered God's help if we trust Him with what concerns us.

pray these words

Lord, I believe in You: increase my faith. I trust in You: strengthen my trust. I love You: let me love You more and more. I am sorry for my sins: deepen my sorrow. I worship You as my first beginning, I long for You as my last end, I praise

You as my constant Helper, and call on You as my loving Protector. Guide me by Your wisdom, correct me with Your justice, comfort me with Your mercy, protect me with Your power. I offer You, Lord, my thoughts: to be fixed on You; my words: to have You for their theme; my actions: to reflect my love for You; my sufferings: to be endured for Your greater glory. I want to do what You ask of me: in the way You ask, for as long as You ask, because You ask it. Lord, enlighten my understanding, strengthen my will, purify my heart, and make me holy. Amen.

                                    ℁ Clement A.D. 95[53]

day 18

FORGET the former things; do not dwell on the past.
Isaiah 43:18

What if you woke up each day and couldn't remember anything that happened the day before? Would you feel as though you were living in a movie like *Groundhog Day* or *50 First Dates?*

This feeling is reality for a Brit named Michelle, who wakes up every morning believing it is 1994. That is the last year vivid in her memory because of anterograde amnesia. Injuries suffered in two auto accidents twenty years ago caused her memory to be wiped clean every single day. She knows her husband, Ian, because they met in 1985, but each day he must show her their 1997 wedding album in order to convince her they are actually married.

Though played to humorous effect in the movies, this life can actually be quite sad and devastating for someone living it. In a recent interview, Michelle admitted, "Right at the beginning for me, it was heartbreaking, knowing that I was different. I didn't want to be different. I wanted to be back to the normal me and not this shell of a person. I want my career back. I want to be able to remember."[54]

We usually think of *forget* as a negative word, but today we take a positive step to *forget the former things*. God calls us to make a choice not to dwell on what has happened in the past, but to embrace life today.

Michelle's condition forces her to begin each day new.

We must simply *choose* to do it.

Too often we cannot let go of regrets, bad choices, and videos that seem to play over and over again on the screen of our minds. But God is greater than our histories. He can help us move to a point where what happened before need not destroy us.

One Bible teacher says, "Of course, we'll face, and many times reap, the consequences of the past. But for the child of God, there is hope. No matter what has happened in our backgrounds, with God there is grace, peace, and hope, if we'll run to Him and bring every past disappointment captive to faith in His Word."[55]

Rahab was a woman who would have loved to *forget* her past.

We meet her in Joshua 2 where she is described as a harlot who runs an inn within the walls of Jericho. Helping Joshua's two spies escape, she pleads for their God to have mercy when the battle comes. Because of her brave and caring acts, she and her family alone are delivered into safety by Joshua during the battle of Jericho (Joshua 6).

We later discover in the New Testament (Matthew 1:5) that Rahab was the mother of Boaz and thus, improbable as it may seem, in the lineage of Jesus.

But what of her life in between?

What amazing acts of grace and mercy propel someone with such a lurid history to change into a woman worthy of being the great-grandmother of the Messiah? My friend Tessa Afshar beautifully weaves Rahab's transformation story into her novel *Pearl in the Sand.*

Rahab is eager to move on beyond her past life, especially when she falls in love with Salome, a godly man who knows all about her and still loves her. And yet she is filled with shame and guilt and cannot forget. So much has changed in her life, yet she feels shackled by the sins of her past.

It is only when she loses one of her treasured pearl earrings that the message finally comes through.

Discovering the jewel buried in the sand, her husband says, "It's no good anymore. It's been lying in the sand a whole night and day. See the mark of the footsteps? It's been trampled on again and again. It's ruined."

But Rahab objects, "No, it's not! I can see it's fine. It needs a careful washing perhaps, but it will be good as new as soon as I give it some proper care."

"People have stepped on it, I tell you; It's worthless now."

"Of course it isn't. Jewels don't lose their value just because they're dirty. It's still a pearl even if it's been stepped on…. Why are you acting this way?"

"You *are* this earring…. Don't you see God looks upon you the way you look upon this delicate jewel? Only with so much more tenderness and delight. You may have been discarded by your father, but that has not robbed you of your true worth. You may have been stepped on by many others, but that has not changed who and what you are, a child of God, made in His image."[56]

Like Rahab, we are not perfect, but we can be cleansed and used by God for amazing ends, if we embrace God's fresh beginnings in our lives. Joseph had a prison record but became prime minister of Egypt. Moses was a murderer but delivered his nation from slavery. Peter openly denied his Lord only to later become God's great voice of the early church. Paul persecuted many Christ-followers before he became a committed missionary to bring the world to Christ.

And yet you say you cannot *forget* what you did because God never forgets? "The files of heaven are filled with stories of redeemed, refitted renegades and rebels.... God is not only willing but pleased to use any vessel—just as long as it is clean today. It may be cracked or chipped. It may be worn or may have never been used before. You can count on this—the past ended one second ago. From this point onward, you can be clean, filled with His Spirit, and used in many different ways for His honor."[57]

What about Michelle? Psychiatrists say that her case is different from most amnesia in that she retains day-to-day skills of how to function in life—but without the social memories. She can carry out everyday things like driving a car and having a conversation. She is able to live a full life each day.

When we choose not to dwell on the past, we discover we can function even better by living and embracing the present and looking forward to the future.

live these words

Later in the same chapter as today's verse we read, "...I alone—will blot out your sins for my own sake and will never think of them again" (Isaiah 43:25 NLT). Perhaps that promise is what prompted Corrie ten Boom to say, "Jesus takes your sin—past, present and future—dumps it in the ocean and puts up a sign that reads, 'No Fishing Allowed!'" About twenty years ago I took her advice literally while at a clergy couples retreat on the Maryland shore. After spending a whole afternoon writing down every sin I could imagine and confessing them to God, I wrapped the papers around a large rock. I walked to the end of a long pier and with all the strength I could muster, I threw that stone into the Chesapeake Bay. As tears ran down my cheeks I could almost see that "No Fishing Allowed" sign. I keep a postcard photo of that pier on my desk.

Of course, in the intervening years, I have fished out some of my past and remembered my regrets. It's almost impossible to truly *forget,* isn't it? That's why I suggest you positively focus on the rest of today's verse, "It is nothing compared to what I am going to do. For I am about to do something new. See, I have already begun! Do you not see it? I will make a pathway through the wilderness. I will create rivers in the dry wasteland" (Isaiah 43:18-19 NLT). Look ahead to what God is about to do in your life. Give names to those *pathways* and *rivers* He is creating. And move forward.

pray these words

Thank You for making it possible to forget any negative images from my past that can hinder my spiritual and personal growth. Thank You that although I can't entirely erase the old, negative images in my memory, I can overpower them with something better. By deliberate choices I can implant positive and realistic images that are inline with what You say about us. You make it possible for me to say and experience what Paul did: 'I focus on this one thing: Forgetting the past and looking forward to what lies ahead, I press on to reach the end of the race and receive the heavenly prize for which God, through Christ Jesus, is calling us' (Philippians 3:13-14 NLT). Amen.

                                ℰ Ruth Myers (1928-2010)[58]

Day 19

sing

SING to the LORD a new song, for He has done
marvelous things…. Psalm 98:1

Does your mother know that lady she's sitting next
to? Cause they're both singing along with the finale of
'There's No Business Like Show Business,'" the head usher
asked my daughter Maggie, who happened to be the female
lead in this musical.

"No, they just met. My mama is *very* friendly,"
Maggie replied with a smile as she walked onstage for her
second bow.

Yes, I *was* singing with the woman next to me. Why
not?

As I had settled into my seat for a third viewing of
Annie Get Your Gun in so many days, I happened to glance

next to me where my seat companion was holding a playbill unlike my own. Hers was also *Annie Get Your Gun,* but from a 1974 performance.

Of course, I had to start a conversation only to find out she had been Annie Oakley then and had come today with her entire ensemble of actresses from thirty-nine years ago! They took up the whole row. After telling her that my daughter was Annie in today's production, we both settled in to enjoy the show, inevitably ending with singing during the bows.

I love to sing, but I'm not a singer.

My daughter Maggie, however, is a professional singer, actor, and dancer in New York, currently starring in an off-Broadway show. And I'm not surprised at all.

When I watch her perform on stage, I'm reminded of three-year-old Maggie dancing on the stage (our fireplace hearth) and singing into a microphone (wooden spoon) "Stop, in the Name of Love."

God gifts each of us individually, and sometimes the gifting is in music.

Though it may come naturally, someone with musical talent still needs to be trained and polished and disciplined along the way in order to offer back the very best to the Giver. The process can be grueling at times—dealing with everything from nodes on the vocal cords to envy among the cast.

But it's worth it if they sing ultimately for the One who *has done marvelous things.* I'm grateful there are many Christians in the arts seeking to live honorably by singing *a new song.*

I'm also grateful there are people who *sing* simply because they want to glorify God.

I love to hear children singing spontaneously while they are playing, walking along the path, even riding in a grocery cart. There is no guile, no sense of embarrassment, but simply a joy overflowing into music. As bystanders break into smile around them, who would argue that lifting our hearts in song isn't contagious?

As far back as the twelfth century, German Christian mystic Hildegarde encouraged those around her to sing out of a grateful heart. "Don't let yourself forget that God's grace rewards not only those who never slip, but also those who bend and fall. So sing! The song of rejoicing softens hard hearts. It makes tears of godly sorrow flow from them. Singing summons the Holy Spirit. Happy praises offered in simplicity and love lead the faithful to complete harmony, without discord. Don't stop singing."[59]

Not only does our Scripture today encourage us to *sing*, but the entire book of Psalms is a believer's songbook. Woven throughout are both laments and praises of a people who lived just like us, weathering life's joys and tragedies. Some of these people were not trained musicians; they simply pulled out every possible instrument (including their voices) and offered back musical worship to their God, who alone is worthy.

But perhaps most puzzling to many of us are the "songs in the night"—that incredible story, found in Acts 16, when Paul and Silas chose to sing and not scream while chained in a Roman prison. They had been stripped and beaten, yet even in the midst of such torture, they drew out of the depths of their being musical praise to the God who was with them in that dark cell.

They choose to *do* something and that something was to *sing*.

The ramifications change heaven and earth as God sends an earthquake to release them from prison and to draw prisoners and warden to the Source of this music.

Back in 1869, Robert Lowry wrote a hymn to remind others to make the same choice.

What though my joys and comforts die? The Lord my Savior liveth; What though the darkness gather round! Songs in the night He giveth: No storm can shake my inmost calm, While to that refuge clinging; Since Christ is Lord of heaven and earth, How can I keep from singing?[60]

I sing aloud every single day.

My morning devotions always include at least one hymn—rich in meaning and comforting in familiar tunes. And I often close a speaking presentation with a musical call to prayer, ending by singing over the people to whom I have just spoken.

I've simply lived long enough now to not care so much about missing a note or sounding breathy. My songs are for an audience of One, and if you happen to be listening in, no problem.

Why? *How can I keep from singing?*

live these words

I realize you are worried that I'm going to suggest you burst into song at your next staff meeting. Well, not exactly. I do believe, however, that all of us could sing a bit more in the course of our daily lives. Open up your hymnal in the morning or evening and sing a favorite, reflecting on the richness of truth in the lyrics. Perhaps you will find yourself singing spontaneously, most certainly to bring smiles and more.

pray these words

God of majesty, whom saints and angels delight to worship in heaven: Be with Your servants who make art and music for Your people, that with joy we on earth may glimpse Your beauty; and bring us to the fulfillment of that hope of perfection which will be ours as we stand before Your unveiled glory. We pray in the name of Jesus Christ our Lord. Amen.

৪০ Book of Common Prayer [61]

day 20

forgive

...*FORGIVE* one another if any of you has a grievance against someone. Forgive as the Lord forgave you.
Colossians 3:13

I read today that our former senior pastor had been relieved of his job by the church board. Without knowing any details, it made me very, very sad.

I was reminded of what happened two dozen years ago.

My husband had served at his first associate pastorate, but it did not end well. After only a year in that role, Mike had found it increasingly difficult to navigate ministry within the bounds of what seemed to us an unhealthy church leadership. So, in order to cause the least amount of church disruption, Mike made the hard decision to take us in a new direction.

And inwardly I blamed everyone for ruining my little family's life.

The previous year we had arrived with our four children (including a newborn) and jumped headlong into a new church family, new state, new schools, and neighborhood. We poured out our lives for the wonderful people there and supported this vibrant, growing church on every level. But, like a divorce for reasons of irreconcilable differences, a few felt we were somehow not a good fit.

And we never saw it coming.

I have never talked about this. The pain and feelings of betrayal by fellow Christians cut so deeply I often wondered if I could ever forgive.

Sadly, the consequences of that uprooting were far-reaching into our whole family—financially, emotionally, and spiritually.

When my kids struggled with having to move to yet another state and high school, it was easy to blame our former church for not being a safe place. In mulling over cause and effect, I regretted our honesty in sharing how God's grace had met us in some struggles. Perhaps they weren't ready for that kind of transparency.

Nonetheless, I did, eventually, *forgive* the church leadership for how they handled our situation. I *had* to forgive in order to move forward into my own new life.

But I struggled with the process, at times turning my anger inward and giving way to despair.

Forgiveness is always a process and a release. In fact, the New Testament Greek word in this scripture is *aphiemi,* which means primarily "to forgive, send away or release the penalty when someone wrongs you." That's why

142

I needed to *release* my desire to hear "I'm sorry," as well as *release* my right to hold onto bitterness or to get even. I simply had to learn to live with the scales unbalanced.

While this is hard to do on my own, it is not impossible with God's help.

When we left, dear friend Genelda's farewell gift was a carefully cross-stitched promise, "...my grace is sufficient for you, for my power is made perfect in weakness" (2 Corinthians 12:9). That plaque hung on the wall of the parsonage where we landed. We christened the new house "Gracehaven."

When we moved in, I pleaded with God to allow us to live there long enough for our three eldest kids to finish high school. In His grace, He actually gave us twenty years in that house, years of learning to embrace grace and welcome others into it.

Someone once defined unforgiveness as "the poison we drink hoping another will die." That may sound crazy, but it is, unfortunately, all too true in the lives of many. Whenever we hold tightly to an unforgiving spirit, we are slowly dying to truth and righteousness.

While we are commanded to "...forgive what others have done to you" (Mark 11:25 CEV), it is important to understand what forgiveness actually does and does not involve. The authors of *Restoring Broken Things* point out some truths that may help clarify what we are seeking.

     ⅋ Forgiveness is not forgetting or ignoring an offense.

     ⅋ Forgiveness is not excusing, justifying, or pardoning an offense.

     ⅋ Forgiveness is not smothering a conflict.

- Forgiveness is not tolerating what should not be tolerated.

- Forgiveness does not always result in reconciliation.

- Forgiveness does not mean you stop hurting.

- Forgiveness is refusing to punish.

- Forgiving is a commitment not to repeat or discuss the matter with others.

- Forgiving is a radical commitment to uproot any residual bitterness.

- Forgiving is a choice to be merciful as God your Father has been merciful with you.[62]

Remember that forgiving someone does not always mean you have to maintain a relationship with them. So far, though I have never had occasion to return to that former city, we continue to exchange annual Christmas cards with fellow staff and friends. Regardless of another's response (or lack of it), forgiveness must propel us forward.

In our verse today, we are reminded that we *forgive* because the Lord forgave us. When I ask God to reveal my own need of His forgiveness, I recall many times I have chosen to go my way, not His—which is, of course, sin.

C. S. Lewis said, "To be a Christian is to forgive the inexcusable, because God has forgiven the inexcusable in me." Thus, when I come to Him in repentance, He offers me a fresh start.

When our world as we knew it came to a crashing

halt, we couldn't help but wonder what God was up to. How would He bring *beauty from ashes*? And yet He did.

I've often taught my children that God leads through closed doors as well as open doors. When the door closed on that ministry, God opened a new door at a remarkable 356-year-old vibrant church in Connecticut. We gratefully entered, though somewhat wounded.

Mike's ministry at our current church has lasted twenty-three years so far, working with three different senior pastors. Imagine! Our four children went through excellent schools and have all now been launched into their own lives out in the world, two daughters having married here at their wonderful home church.

Does God honor our efforts at moving beyond our pain into pursuing a new life and new endeavors? Absolutely.

But it will never happen if we don't first do the hard work of *forgiving*.

live these words

Is there someone you need to forgive in order for you to move more unencumbered through life? Stop drinking that poison! Here is an exercise that I have found to be helpful in such situations: Picture yourself kneeling at the foot of the cross and carefully laying each grievance at the feet of Jesus. Pray a prayer for each person or situation as you release the pain, leaving the consequences in His capable hands. Then never pick it up!

pray these words

Lord Jesus, thank You for caring about how much my heart has been hurt. You know the pain

I have felt because of (list every offense). Right now I release all that pain into Your hands. Thank You, Lord, for dying on the cross for me and extending Your forgiveness to me. As an act of my will, I choose to forgive (name). Right now I move (name) off my back to Yours. I refuse all thoughts of revenge. I trust that in Your time and in Your way You will deal with (name) as You see fit. And Lord, Thank You for giving me Your power to forgive so that I can be set free. In Your precious name I pray. Amen.

ℛ June Hunt[63]

day 21

proclaim

...*PROCLAIM* the message; be persistent whether the time is favorable or unfavorable; convince, rebuke, and encourage, with the utmost patience in teaching.

2 Timothy 4:2 NRSV

*U*nderstudy. Replacement. Substitute. Interim.

Have you ever been called upon to take someone else's place at the very last minute? Rarely convenient—always a stretch.

John wasn't a preacher. But this layman was prepared to proclaim the message as needed. As a deacon in the Primitive Methodist Chapel of Colchester, England, he had a simple faith and a willing spirit. Sometimes that's all that is required.

On this particular January Sunday in 1850, John awakened to a world of white. Though many were snowed in, he didn't seem to think that God took snow days, so he put on his boots and trudged six miles into town for church.

Not surprisingly, the church crowd was sparse that day—twelve members and one visitor, a thirteen-year old boy. In fact, the preacher wasn't even able to make it due to the snow, so someone suggested they cancel the service. After all, who would give the sermon? Being the only church officer in attendance, John Egglen volunteered to do the honors, based on the scheduled text of Isaiah 45:22, "Look to Me, and be saved, All you ends of the earth! For I am God, and there is no other" (NKJV).

But remember, he was no preacher.

In fact, he stammered and verbally wandered for about ten minutes until he fixed his eyes on the stranger, easily distinguished in the little company, and said, "Young man, you look very miserable."

The blow struck home, and although the young man had never had such a personal word from the pulpit before, he listened intently.

John continued, "You always will be miserable— miserable in life and miserable in death—if you don't obey my text; but if you obey now, this moment you will be saved." Then, lifting up his hands, he shouted, as only a Primitive Methodist of that time could, "Young man, look to Jesus Christ! Look! Look! Look! You have nothin' to do but to look and live."[64]

I'm not a preacher either, but there have certainly been times when I have needed to step in and proclaim, whether the time is favorable or unfavorable. I will never

148

forget receiving an invitation to speak at the opening chapel on my first day of seminary—a time when women were still somewhat rare in such circles. For some reason, out of the entire first-year class, this Boston school chose me and another guy from Carolina to bring a word to fellow students just embarking on our course of theological training.

Honestly, to this day I do not remember *what* I said. But I do remember that I *said* it with conviction and Holy Spirit power.

God's words to Jeremiah were the promise I clung to back then. "Do not say, 'I am only a youth,' for you will go to everyone I send you to and speak whatever I tell you" (Jeremiah 1:7 HCSB). While I am definitely no longer a youth, I still find courage to proclaim truth through God's power and anointing.

As I pray for guidance, He literally puts the words in my mouth. Like our verse says, sometimes those words need to convict or rebuke, so we must rely heavily on God's grace in the speaking of them.

Personally, I prefer it when those words I am called to proclaim are words of encouragement.

We never know where our words will land, do we? Canadian Pastor Mark Buchanan, in his book *The Rest of God,* elaborates, "I'd delight if none of my words fell to the ground—if none were useless, excessive, dispensable, easily dismissed…. But that's God's business…. Either God, God alone, keeps our words from falling and scatters them wide, or else there is nothing in them worth keeping and scattering in the first place. Our concern, our responsibility, is simply to hear and heed God."[65]

What about John Egglen's words that were proclaimed that snowy day so long ago? Did they make a difference to that small congregation?

Well, as that teenage boy recalled many years later, they most certainly did, "I had this vision—not a vision to my eyes, but to my heart. I saw what a Savior Christ was.... Now I can never tell you how it was, but I no sooner saw whom I was to believe than I also understood what it was to believe, and I did believe in one moment.

"And as the snow fell on my road home from the little house of prayer, I thought every snowflake talked with me and told of the pardon I had found, for I was white as the driven snow through the grace of God."[66]

That teenager's name? Charles Haddon Spurgeon.

Known today as England's Prince of Preachers.

live these words

Tradition has it that Saint Francis once said, "Preach the Gospel always. If necessary, use words." Do you suppose that was a mandate for us to *do* the Gospel and not just *proclaim* it? What do you most remember after hearing a good sermon? Chances are, it's the stories that take hold of your heart and provide a lasting influence.

Jesus taught through stories, too. Whether or not we are preachers, the world is watching and listening to those who have chosen to live for Christ. What story does He want you to share? Why not spend some time preparing for your own snowy day?

pray these words

Dear Lord, You have sent me into this world to proclaim Your word. So often the problems of the world seem so complex and intricate that Your word strikes me as embarrassingly simple. Many times I feel tongue-tied in the company of people who are dealing with the world's social and economic problems. But You, O Lord, said, 'Be clever as serpents and innocent as doves.' Let me retain innocence and simplicity in the midst of this complex world...What really counts is that all this information, knowledge and insight allow me to speak more clearly and unambiguously Your truthful word. Do not allow evil powers to seduce me with the complexities of the world's problems, but give me the strength to think clearly, speak freely, and act boldly in Your service. Amen.

                              ∞ Henri Nouwen (1932-1996)[67]

day 22

receive

...RECEIVE power when the Holy Spirit comes on you....
Acts 1:8

*M*y first thought was, *What am I doing sprawled at the bottom of these stairs?*

Beside me, I noticed my purse in the corner and one shoe lying nearby.

I didn't know exactly how I had fallen down the stairs, but as I was bundled off into an ambulance, I knew I was in big trouble.

My mind raced with the ambulance.

I thought about how great the weekend conference had been going and how well-received my first two presentations had been. I remembered eager anticipation of a free afternoon exploring the quaint Amish countryside.

A trip to the emergency room had not been on my agenda.

Now here I was, injured in an unfamiliar city. Tears streamed down my face as I prayed for God to help guide me and be with me in this strange hospital.

God's promise "Fear not, for I *am* with you" (Isaiah 43:5 NKJV) calmed me during the hours of treatment for a broken leg and the dread that engulfed me after hearing I'd be immobilized all of November and December.

"So, what's the subject of your talk tonight?" the technician teased after she had heard my story.

"God's Presence in the midst of suffering," I weakly replied, the irony all too apparent.

After vulnerably receiving lots of help in getting dressed later that evening, I rolled into the meeting room and invited the ladies to gather around my wheelchair.

"Let's have a fireside chat about Christ's presence in the midst of our suffering," I said. Armed with power from on high and a slight dose of painkillers, I found the strength to speak and pray with them all evening.

My pain subsided. I sensed new power go through my words, but more importantly, a peace came through my willingness to be a living example of a surrendered soul. My natural responses of panic and worry faded, replaced by serenity and trust.

And it felt like Jesus was holding my hand the next day during the difficult flight home to my long convalescence.

Soon after I returned home, a beautiful potholder quilt made by all the conferees arrived with this note, "Thanks for showing us the power of the Holy Spirit to persevere and be used even when the going gets tough."

I believe that "His [God's] divine power has given us everything we need..." (2 Peter 1:3) for all the unexpected things that come our way. Yes, the Holy Spirit, the third person of the Trinity, is available to every believer. But that doesn't mean we always choose to live in that power. It is up to us to willingly *receive* it.

The power and strength of God alive within us by His Holy Spirit and the revelation of that truth releases spiritual power in our lives, which strengthens both our bodies and spirits. The Greek word *dunamis* is often used in reference to the power of the Holy Spirit available to us. This word is the root word for dynamic, dynamo, and dynamite. Dynamite power, by way of the Holy Spirit, enables us to be dynamic witnesses, more than conquerors (spiritual dynamos), and stronger people.

Think about vacuuming. If you push and pull the vacuum back and forth across your carpet, it may leave trails through the fibers that make your floor appear clean, but if you don't plug your vacuum in to the electricity, no dirt is removed. The same is true of your life—you need to plug into the power.

When we are truly plugged in to the power of the Holy Spirit, there are significant changes in our lives—primarily, we have a new desire to magnify and glorify God through worship and also a powerful disposition to obey God in everyday life.

How is God glorified? His glory is revealed each time one of His followers is divinely empowered to be or do something we could never do on our own. As we recognize this power is from God through the Holy Spirit, we glorify Him.

Paul said, "...we have this treasure in jars of clay to show that this all-surpassing power is from God and not from us" (2 Corinthians 4:7). When God uses me to help someone discover new spiritual strength, I absolutely know it is a direct result of the Holy Spirit power working through me, because I am so aware of how ordinary and chipped my own clay jar is.

Pastor Mark Batterson puts it this way: "The anointing [of Holy Spirit power] is the difference between what you can do and what God can do. It's the place where the power of God and the favor of God intersect. It's the difference between the natural and the supernatural. It's the difference between the temporal and the eternal. It's the difference between success and failure."[68]

I spent way too much time attempting great things for God through my own efforts. Sort of like trying to clean with that unplugged vacuum. Sure, I kicked up a bit of dust, but nothing of lasting value ever came of it.

Our verse today is from that amazing anointing at Pentecost when so many *received* Holy Spirit power. Those first-century Christians were so filled that they turned the world upside down. "That power changed them from fearful men [and women] to radiant witnesses for Christ. They were used of God to change the course of history. And the same omnipotent power, the power of the Holy Spirit, is available to you to enable you to live a holy and fruitful life for Jesus Christ."[69]

Open your hands. Open your heart. Prepare to be filled.

And then, watch out, world!

live these words

Are you tired of trying to live an unlimited life with only limited power? In order to receive from God, we must always come before Him in a posture of repentance and humility, confessing that all too often we have chosen to go solo. In Ephesians 5:18 we are told to "...be filled with the Spirit...." The actual verb used means "to be continually filled every day."

Our part is to pray to God for His power, His purpose, His provision for all that will come our way. If the prayer to be filled doesn't bring on an emotional experience, we should not be concerned. As you continue to inhale God's Spirit and exhale His power, you will discover much more adventure and ability to follow through with all He sends your way.

Perhaps the Spirit is nudging you to say "yes" to that volunteer position you were offered. You don't feel adequate and you aren't sure you're ready. But the nudging doesn't go away. Perhaps it is time to claim the full power and go for it. Only God can reveal His plan to you.

Remember, even clay pots can shine brightly for His glory. It all depends on what is inside.

pray these words

O Holy Spirit, as the sun is full of light, the ocean full of water, Heaven full of glory, so may my heart be full of Thee. Vain are all divine purposes of love and the redemption wrought by Jesus except Thou work within, regenerating by Thy power, giving me eyes to see Jesus, showing me the realities of the unseen world. Give me Thyself without measure, as an unimpaired fountain, as inexhaustible riches. Suffer me not to grieve or resist Thee. Come as Power, to expel every rebel lust, to reign supreme and keep me

Thine; Come as Teacher, leading me into all truth, filling me with all understanding; Come as Love, that I may adore the Father, and love Him as my all; Come as Joy, to dwell in me, move in me, animate me; Come as Light, illuminating the Scripture, moulding me in its laws; Come as Sanctifier, body, soul and spirit wholly Thine; Come as Helper, with strength to bless and keep, directing my every step. Magnify to me Thy glory by being magnified in me...Amen.

ᔕ Puritan Prayer[70]

day 23

give

GIVE, and it will be given to you. A good measure, pressed down, shaken together and running over, will be poured into your lap. Luke 6:38

Where have you been, Justin?" I asked my son when I finally caught up with him at his nearby apartment.

"Oh, I heard Dr. Bill was sick so I made him a casserole. It only took me about half an hour to walk there," he replied cheerfully.

"Wow, hon, that was so thoughtful. What did you cook?"

"I made macaroni and cheese, and they loved it. Besides, that's just what you *do*—take food to church friends who are sick."

Justin, a young adult with intellectual disabilities, sees the world in very clear terms. When someone is in need, we *give*. This was only the latest example.

158

People are frequently informing me how pleased they were when my son volunteered to help them move, or mow the lawn, or shovel snow. Though he is on a fixed income, he always donates to mission trips and buys children's gifts for the Angel Tree and Shoebox outreach at Christmas. Some Sundays I sit next to him in the pew and watch him empty his pocket of change to fill the offering envelope; other times he inserts his biggest bill.

I know that if God loves a cheerful giver, He must really cherish Justin.

Too bad the act of giving isn't as clear a mandate for everyone. I admit that when I hear of someone in need, I don't always automatically switch into action.

Jesus encouraged us to *give*, not only if there is extra money sitting around, but even when we are barely making it financially. While sitting in the temple and watching many people bring their offerings, he noticed a poor widow whose offering was a meager two coins. In order to emphasize the spirit of giving, Jesus said, "This poor widow has given more than all the rest of them. For they have given a tiny part of their surplus, but she, poor as she is, has given everything she has" (Luke 21: 3-4 NLT).

Famous eighteenth-century preacher John Wesley didn't only talk about helping others, he put his intentions into a lifestyle. In his sermon "The Use of Money," he encouraged folks to "Make all you can. Save all you can. Give all you can."

And then he lived that way. "The genesis of Wesley's generosity was a covenant he made with God in 1731. He decided to limit his expenses so he had more margin to give.... Wesley's goal was to give away all excess income after bills were paid and family needs were taken care of.... He believed that God's blessings should result in us raising not our *standard of living* but our *standard of giving*. Wesley continued to raise his standard of giving. Even when his income rose into the thousands of pounds, he lived simply and gave away all surplus money. He died with a few coins in his pocket but a storehouse of treasure in heaven."[71]

Many people say this is an impossible way to live in the twenty-first century. To that I would lift up the example of Randy Alcorn and his *Treasure Principle*—"You can't take it with you, but you can send it on ahead."

"The keys to living this principle are all rooted in Scripture.

1. God owns everything. I'm His money manager.
2. My heart always goes where I put God's money.
3. Heaven, not Earth, is my home. We are citizens of a better country.
4. Giving is the only antidote to materialism.
5. God prospers me not to raise my standard of living but to raise my standard of giving."[72]

My other son, Tim, who lives in the Pacific Northwest, guides his giving by these same principles. I'm grateful for his example of a young adult who has chosen to tithe regularly, both through his finances and also volunteering service at several local charities and Christian ministries. And he even kept doing this during a time of unemployment in the recession a few years ago.

Compared to most of the world, each person who is reading this book is considered wealthy. Most of us have all we need and more. Gratitude should thus compel us to *give* and to do it in a joy-filled way.

> Each of you should give what you have decided in your heart to give, not reluctantly or under compulsion, for God loves a cheerful giver (2 Corinthians 9:7).

This week I had lunch with a *cheerful giver* who also happens to be a *New York Times* bestselling author many times over. When I asked her about her dreams and vision for the future, she replied, "To be able to give $10 million a year to God's work...," casually adding, "without having to die!" I honestly believe she will meet that dream one day. She is well on her way, and greatly inspiring folks like me in the process.

While we don't give for the purpose of being blessed in turn, it is amazing how God's economy tends to balance the scales. Justin lives a frugal and simple life. But catastrophe hit last summer—all his belongings were ruined when a major thunderstorm caused raw sewage to flood his basement apartment. After NBC News and the Connecticut Health Department left the scene, Mike and I wondered how we could help our son through this upheaval. In addition to needing all new furniture and many household items that had been destroyed, he also needed a new apartment and a real source of emotional peace.

Because of the news broadcast, we never even had to ask anyone for help.

Within hours, people began to mobilize, and I received emails and phone calls with offers of sofas, desk, computer, tables, chairs, bed, gift cards, and physical help for moving. An even more suitable second-floor apartment miraculously became available in the same complex. Within weeks, *all* his needs had been met through gracious givers, mostly people who had at one time been on the receiving end of Justin's good will.

A *good measure, pressed down, shaken together and running over* was literally poured into his lap.

When we act in love and generosity to others, it spills over to our own lives. "You can give without loving, but you cannot love without giving. If you really love someone, you will give till it hurts. Jesus certainly did."[73]

live these words

If we don't have a plan for giving, we probably won't end up giving. Grow as a giver by deciding to tithe at least 10 percent of your income or "strive to tithe." Give first to your own church community, but also take part in supporting missionaries, sponsoring children, organizations that help in crises, local food banks, and even secular charities whose cause you can fully endorse. Consider offering your time for a local building project or a short-term mission trip. If you can't go yourself, help with and support the fundraisers so others can go. Write down your giving plans for the year. Consider taking a vacation with a difference, where you travel somewhere and help with a project instead of as a tourist. For a milestone birthday, ask friends and family to give to a special need. Be creative. No matter what amount of money you have to give away, there are many others whose lives will change because you do it.

pray these words

Lord Jesus, regarding my money and resources: do they own my heart, or am I stewarding them well? Your words are ringing in my heart today —where my treasure is, there is my heart also. Where is my heart today, Lord? I submit to Your loving embrace and Your honest evaluation. Where the things of this world have a grip on my heart, help me to release them. Where I value my possessions more than I honor You, the Lord of all, forgive me and grant me Your compassion. Where I long for things that have been created more than You, the Creator of all things, grant me Your peace. I want my heart to treasure that which You treasure, Lord. May it be so today, for You and You alone are the center of my heart and the lover of my soul. In Jesus' name. Amen.

                              ❧ Stephen A. Macchia[74]

day 24

clothe

...*CLOTHE* yourselves with compassion, kindness, humility, gentleness and patience. Colossians 3:12

We get dressed every day. Occasionally, twice in a day. Depending on our personality and the occasion, we sometimes give a lot of thought and attention to what we wear. It took me months to find an appropriate mother-of-the-bride gown. Twice.

Other times, we throw something on without thinking. Just grab the nearest sweater and comfy jeans and we're good to go.

We wouldn't dream of not being clothed.

That's why Paul knew he would have our attention by using this imagery—to *clothe* ourselves. Except he doesn't complete the sentence with the expected words of what to put on like cloak, sandals, or robe. He throws in a twist.

He tells us to get dressed up in *kindness*. To button up *gentleness,* and step into *patience.*

Well, what in the world does *that* look like?

Earlier in this letter to the believers living in Colossae, Paul reminded them that they are new creatures in Christ. Referring to the ways they used to walk, he suggests they get rid of *(take off)* a long list of unholy practices, and then *put on the new self"*(Colossians 3:7-10).

Before the new clothing is listed, Paul reiterates the most important truth of all—they are "chosen, holy, and dearly loved" by God (verse 12). Embracing these facts is key because our identity always precedes our actions and attitudes. We are new creatures through our faith in Christ, by no merit of our own, who have a significant role to play.

We must decide to put on Christ each day, just as we put on clothing. Henri Nouwen observes, "Being a believer means being clothed in Christ. This is much more than wearing a cloak.... It refers to a total transformation."

When we freely choose to dress in spiritual clothes every day, the Holy Spirit produces change—change in our personalities, our priorities, and our prayer. What is alive in our hearts shines out from us.

The five "garments" mentioned in today's verse are what I would call somewhat muted clothing. They don't make a huge splash, like bright jewel colors and bling, but are instead lovely and quite powerful in their subtle beauty.

> ๛ Compassion (Greek word *oiktirmos*: meaning "mercy, feeling sympathy for others' misfortunes")—as we wear compassion we will be better able to come alongside those who are in pain and trouble.

- Kindness (Greek word *chrestotes:* meaning "to extend goodwill, kindness, and helpfulness") —those who wear kindness are quick to offer help and a good word to anyone.

- Humility (Greek word *tapeinophrosyne*: meaning "a lowliness of mind and attitude, modesty") – when we wear humility, we are content to work in the background, not calling attention to ourselves.

- Gentleness (Greek word *proutes*: describing "meekness, obedient submissiveness to God") —clothed in gentleness, we are more apt to speak quietly, move slowly, and carry out God's ways in a loving manner.

- Patience (Greek word *makrothumia*: which means "long-suffering, handling injustice or difficulty well")—those who wear patience will always be welcome as a tribute to fortitude and serenity in the midst of the unknown.

If we truly incorporated these garments into our daily wardrobe, would they change the way we live? Once again, Jesus' own life provides a clear answer. Here is the creative way Walter Wangerin describes the passion in his story "Ragman."

A man follows a ragman as he walks the city alleys, coming into contact with many street people. When he comes on a crying woman, he offers to exchange his rags for her handkerchief. On receiving hers, he begins to cry, but she is now left with a clean linen cloth and no tears. Then he comes on a girl whose head is wrapped in a bloody cloth. When he gives her a clean, new yellow bonnet, he takes her rags and soon begins to bleed from his head while also sobbing uncontrollably.

Encountering an amputee, he gives him a new coat, in which each sleeve is filled with an arm. But when the ragman takes the old coat, he is suddenly one-armed. Almost stumbling over a drunk, he covers him with a new blanket and takes the old blanket himself. So now the ragman is a pitiful sight and staggers drunkenly, one-armed, head bleeding, and sobbing toward the landfill at the edge of the city. Yet everyone he encountered is now whole.

The narrator of the story, the witness to the ragman's exchanges, watches him die in the dump and then sleeps for days. When he awakens, he is startled to see the ragman standing up whole again. Except for the scar on his forehead, he is healthy and all the rags are now clean and new.

His response? "Well, then I lowered my head and trembling for all that I had seen, I myself walked up to the Ragman. I told him my name with shame, for I was a sorry figure next to him.

"Then I took off all my clothes in that place, and I said to him with dear yearning in my voice: 'Dress me.'

"He dressed me. My Lord, he put new rags on me, and I am a wonder beside him. The Ragman, the Ragman, the Christ!"[75]

This same "Ragman"—Jesus Christ—promises to take care of us, whatever our need. We can be "clothed in Christ" (Romans 13:14).

So today, as you put on your clothing, remember that you are holy, chosen, and deeply loved. You have taken off the grave clothes and are now putting on grace clothes.

All dressed up with somewhere to go—out into the world.

live these words

On the TV reality show *What Not to Wear,* two fashionistas named Clinton and Stacy invade an unsuspecting person's closet, throwing out everything she loves. Then they show her three mannequins modeling the kind of outfits she should be wearing. They point out colors, styles, lines, and textures that will best compliment her body and her lifestyle, giving her a $5,000 credit card to shop for a whole new wardrobe—on her own. Viewers watch this fashion victim struggle that first day with wanting to use the money to buy newer and nicer versions of her old clothing, rather than the more appropriate styles suggested by the experts. Which brings us to the second day of shopping when the advisers appear at the store and force her to get serious about their new guidelines. She eventually does this, resulting in a new look and the confidence that goes with it.

While watching, I can't help but imagine the apostle Paul going through my spiritual wardrobe and tossing all my favorites in the garbage can. ("Please, not my *impatience* sweater. Don't take my *anger* jeans!") He wants me to totally change my style. In other words, don't go shopping for fresh versions of old clothes; "…you have taken off your old self with its practices and have put on the new self, which is being renewed in knowledge in the image of its Creator" (Colossians 3:9-10).

Why not make a list of the spiritual clothing that needs to be culled from your wardrobe/life? And while you're at it, you could probably do with going through your closet and filling up a huge bag of donations for your Salvation Army store. Once a year my author friends and I gather for

168

an accessory exchange, bringing purses, jewelry, jackets, belts, shoes, scarves, and vests that we are ready to discard. We turn it into a game and have a blast, lovingly praying for our sister as we wear her hand-me-downs.

pray these words

> *O Christ, clothe me with Yourself. Be for me a warm garment that will protect me from catching the cold of this world. If you are away from me, dear Lord, all things will be cold and lifeless. But if You are with me, all things will be warm, lively and fresh. As I cover my body with this article of clothing, please become the clothing of my soul. Put upon me mercy, meekness, love, and peace. Amen.*

> ∞ John Bradford (1510-1535)[76]

day 25

work

...WORK enthusiastically for the Lord, for you know
that nothing you do for the Lord is ever useless.
1 Corinthians 15:58 NLT

Sometimes we work for money. Sometimes we work for love.

Sometimes our work expresses our unique gifting, while other times we perform unfamiliar duties simply out of necessity. Many times we never know the long-term results of our endeavors, but that shouldn't prevent us from giving our all to the task at hand.

I was thinking of all these things as I sat on the stage next to a huge portrait of Mark Twain and began interviewing an author with the question, "Why would twenty-first-century people want to read a story set in ancient Persia?" Her response had us all spellbound—that people then, as now, struggled with questions such as *Where do I find my worth? How can I be happy when life didn't turn out as I hoped? How do I overcome in the midst of life's battles?* The audience connected with these questions. These were their own questions and they wanted to hear more, so I kept the conversation going as hundreds saw a whole new world opened to them through the message of one book from the heart of one author.

I love what I do.

Actually, I have three part-time jobs—writing, speaking, and teaching. But that night I was simply acting as a conduit so someone else could share her message. This wasn't work-for-money, this was Kingdom work. Investing in others with no guarantee of how God would use my efforts, but simply responding to His call with enthusiasm and obedience.

Months before, our little writers group had been brainstorming—always an interesting prospect. We each bring something different to the table. Lauren is a New York theater critic and playwright, Tessa is a novelist specializing in biblical and historical romance, and I'm a non-fiction author and speaker. We wanted to throw Tessa a book launch for her new novel, but where? Upon investigating libraries, museums, and other event venues we quickly realized we had champagne tastes but only a ginger ale budget. So we prayed, and kept exploring.

Miraculously, Lauren talked the Mark Twain House and Museum in Hartford, Connecticut, into sponsoring their first book launch, "though we can't imagine why anyone would show up to hear a Christian author...." They even agreed to underwrite some expenses, along with the book's Chicago-based publisher. Because Iranian-born Tessa Afshar's *Harvest of Gold* was set in Persia and Jerusalem during Nehemiah's building of the wall, there was a definite connection to Mark Twain's travels in the Middle East as well as his interest in religion.

The director who coordinated various writer events at the museum was quick to point out that previously 150 people had shown up to hear their only other "faithy" author/presenter—an atheist. He may just as well have thrown down the gauntlet for us and said, "Top *that*, will you?"

And so our work began.

Our mission was threefold. 1. Celebrate and publicize the release of Tessa's new novel; 2. Entertain guests with an interesting program and delicious Persian tea reception; 3. Bring the arts and literary community together with Christians who love to read.

I was more than happy to be a greeter and to moderate the interview and Q&A session with the audience. But I also needed to pitch in on other things that were not my forte —like flower arranging. After collecting blue hydrangeas and white roses from the gardens of gracious friends, I spent the afternoon with Tessa putting together eighteen breathtaking arrangements. Those beautiful fresh flowers were God's creation—all we did was *work enthusiastically* to figure out how to feature them.

Lauren and Tessa and Persian friends spent hours tasting and preparing authentic Persian treats such as kashke bademjan (eggplant tapenade), lime and sea salt pistachios, cardamom and rosewater baklava, almond cookies, figs, and pomegranate seeds to go along with our strong black tea.

That evening, 231 people came to the Mark Twain House and Museum for their first book launch—the largest in-house crowd at any of their writer events. Their bookstore sold out of Tessa's personally signed books.

And a good time was had by all! By the end of the cleanup we were exhausted but happy, knowing that *nothing you do for the Lord is ever useless."*

We leave the fruit of our labor in God's hands—His part.

Our part is to work hard. And to remember, as author Robert Benson says, "...the work we do is not actually the center of the universe. The work that we do—whatever hat we are wearing, however great or small it may seem to us or to anyone else at the time—is to be done in the *service* of the Center of the Universe."[77]

A few days after the book launch, Lauren said to me, "Cindy, do you remember that day you and I met to pray over each aspect of the event? Well, I just realized that every single prayer was answered. We even had enough Persian food for the extras who showed up!"

Our same group is now directing a writers retreat up in the New Hampshire mountains. We will again be pioneering something new and working hard.

Somehow I think God will show up.

And that is success. Not numbers, not the opinions of others. Now how many people we please. Just Him.

live these words

What work has God given you to do today? I'm not just talking about your paying job—though if you have one (or several), it's important to use all your integrity and ability as you carry out each responsibility. Are you being stretched into new ventures, perhaps even through volunteer work or ministry? Will you tackle each opportunity with God's help and a prayer that He will provide all you need to accomplish His purpose through you?

Write down three ways you can *work enthusiastically for the Lord* this week, inviting Him to accompany you all the way.

pray these words

> *O God, Your Word tells me that, whatever my hand finds to do, I must do it with might. Help me today to concentrate with my whole attention on whatever I am doing, and keep my thoughts from wandering and my mind from straying. When I am working, help me to work with my whole mind. When I am playing, help me to play with my whole heart. Help me to do one thing at a time and to do it well. This I ask for Jesus' sake. Amen.*

>   William Barclay (1907-1978)[78]

Day 26

ask

...*ASK* for the ancient paths, ask where the good way
is, and walk in it, and you will find rest for your souls.
Jeremiah 6:16

*M*y husband, a Protestant minister in an active church
community, daily prays through the Benedictine
breviary—a prayer book with 1,500 years of prayers from
St. Benedict onward. He also writes (paints) orthodox icons.
Long ago he *asked* for the *ancient paths* and in following
them found not only rest for his soul, but a home for his
worship and service as well.

So naturally, I thought of Mike when six years ago I
happened to meet the contemplative writer Robert Benson
at a bookseller convention. My fellow authors and dinner
companions had pointed him out to me sitting alone in a

restaurant. I was eager to go up and thank him for his latest memoir (honestly, I would gladly read a grocery list written by that man).

In the process, I casually asked him if he had a new book coming out that week, and he told me about his latest, *In Constant Prayer.* As he described it I immediately determined to buy a copy for my husband's birthday that month.

Because, of course, my husband greatly appreciates such things.

When the copy arrived by post, I happened to open it first and peruse it before I giftwrapped it. Soon I had devoured the entire book. Benson's words—encouraging me to pray the daily office—came as a catalyst to set me on the *good way* and changed my life.

"Words are powerful things. Who knows what a single one of them might do to us over time? ...The daily office offers me rich, powerful, profound words that can change me and shape me. Words that have been given as a gift through the ages to me and you. Words that can grow in me and give voice to the groaning of my heart when I cannot. Words that can teach me to be attentive to and to perceive the meaning of the word of God. Words that will lead me into a deeper and deeper communion with God. But not if I do not say them."[79]

Many years ago a pastor challenged me, "When life squeezes you, what words and actions come out?" Squirming in the pew, I thought of such things that spill over at my first sign of stress and decided it was time to clean up— from the inside out.

I began to *ask*—to search—how to be filled and thus live from a healthy overflow in those inevitable life-squeezing moments.

Because what comes out is what's *inside*, friends. The core of who we are is revealed most vividly in such trying times. Jesus reminds us, "...for his mouth speaks from the overflow of the heart" (Luke 6:45).

This is where our power and influence ultimately reside. In the moments of prayer, solitude, worship, Bible study, silence—that's when God gives us what He wants us to pass along to others.

Most of us *believe* in the importance of soul care doctrinally, but how many of us actually carve out significant time each day to build on that which is never seen? How much time, energy, and resources do you spend on maintaining a healthy spiritual center?

Have you ever received one of those dreaded messages informing you that you are overdrawn at the bank? Basically, you spent more money than you had deposited. This same thing happens all too often with our spiritual lives. We get that phone call, medical diagnosis, or pink slip, and all of the sudden we need to draw upon spiritual resources that are simply not there. I cannot emphasize enough the importance of daily deposits into your heart account, also known as spiritual disciplines, which have been borne out by centuries of Christians.

If we don't know about such things, that's because this work takes place out of sight. Where no one sees.

In *The Great Bridge,* David McCullough writes about the building of the tower that became known as the Brooklyn Bridge. Evidently, the public didn't see enough results for all the work their taxes were supporting. So, in June 1872, the chief engineer of the project placed a letter in the newspaper in response to their impatience: "To such of the general public as might imagine that no work had been done on the New York tower, because they see no evidence of it above the water, I should simply remark that the amount of the masonry and concrete laid on the foundation during the past winter, under water, is equal in quantity to the entire masonry of the Brooklyn tower visible today above the waterline."[80]

In other words, the construction team's investment in all that unseen work was integral—building a strong foundation that helped make the Brooklyn Bridge the powerful transportation artery that has stood for the past 140 years.

Will the quiet spiritual work done in your and my souls determine whether or not we will stand the test of time? For some of us, it may not look like much is happening on the outside right now. That's okay if there is foundational work going on, if deposits are being made.

During the past decade, my moment-by-moment deposits and soul care habits have grown and changed. I'm becoming more contemplative as I embrace listening prayer, solitude, and silence. While I continue to pray extemporaneously, I am also treasuring ancient prayers that have been prayed corporately for centuries.

What better way to start the day than with this morning prayer, *Lord God, almighty and everlasting Father, you have brought me in safety to this new day: Preserve me with Your mighty power, that I may not fall into sin, nor be overcome by adversity; and in all I do direct me to the fulfilling of Your purpose; through Jesus Christ my Lord, Amen* (Book of Common Prayer).[81]

178

I usually sing a hymn, the rich theology of the verses ministering to my soul as well as the music. God loves that we make a joyful noise to Him. It is also an important spiritual discipline to sit silently for at least five minutes, awaiting a word from God, which will most assuredly come. But only if we are quiet and receptive for that still small voice.

At the day's end, I once again go to prayer, examine what the day has held, what has been done or undone, and spend time in repentance and confession, committing all to the One who never sleeps. My favorite night prayer is *Keep watch, dear Lord, with all who work or watch or weep this night, and give Your angels charge over those who sleep; Tend the sick, we pray, and give rest to the weary; soothe the suffering and bless the dying: pity the afflicted and shield the joyous; and all for Your love's sake. Amen.* (Book of Common Prayer).[82]

There is a good path for our spiritual journey. And God promises to be with us along the way.

First we have to *ask* directions. And follow them.

live these words

Perhaps it's time to be stretched on your faith journey. Step into something new within the Christian realm. Attend a church worship service that is different from your own, whether in style, language, or denomination. Go to an exhibit of religious art through the centuries or visit a working monastery. If you are not from a liturgical background, try observing the season of Advent (pre-Christmas) or Lent (pre-Easter). There are many seasonal devotionals available to guide you through those forty days. Also *ask* God where you might incorporate different spiritual disciplines into your already scheduled devotional life. Perhaps trying out your first silent retreat or keeping a spiritual journal. The great thing about the life of faith is that we are always discovering new things in God's Word because we are continually growing into new people. Decide today what parts of the *ancient path* you will tread in order to find *rest for your soul*.

pray these words

> *Most merciful God, order my day so that I may know what You want me to do, and then help me to do it. Let me not be elated by success or depressed by failure. I want only to take pleasure in what pleases you, and only to grieve at what displeases You. For the sake of Your love I would willingly forgo all temporal comforts. May all the joys in which You have no part weary me. May all the work which You do not prompt be tedious to me. Let my thoughts frequently turn to You, that I may be obedient to You without complaint, patient without grumbling, cheerful without self-indulgence, contrite without dejections, and serious without solemnity. Let me hold You in awe without feeling terrified of You, and let me be an example to others without any trace of pride. Amen.*

                                            ଚ Thomas Aquinas (1225-1274)[83]

Day 27

weep

...*WEEP* with those who weep. Romans 12:15 ESV

*A*s emcee I realized I had completely lost control of the meeting. But glancing around the room at clusters of women crying softly, I decided I didn't care that this wasn't ending the way we had planned.

Because by now I, too, was crying.

Our gathering of kindred spirit authors had just been told that one of our own, a dear sister, was diagnosed with late-stage cancer. The prognosis was bleak and we were devastated.

All we could do was *weep*.

We were, perhaps without realizing it, entering into an ancient Christian tradition called the *charism of tears*. Saints of old viewed crying as a grace or a gift to be offered to one in pain or grief.

A way to enter in to their sorrow and share it.

I'm reminded of the little girl who lost a playmate in death and one day reported to her family that she had gone to comfort the sorrowing mother.

"What did you say?" asked her father.

"Nothing," she replied. "I just climbed up on her lap and cried with her."

Isn't that exactly what we are told to do—*weep with those who weep*? And yet nothing in our modern culture encourages such behavior. Even in our churches.

Pastor Eugene Peterson observes, "It's an odd thing. Jesus wept. Job wept. David wept. Jeremiah wept. They did it openly. Their weeping became a matter of public record. Their weeping, sanctioned by inclusion in our Holy Scriptures, is a continuing and reliable witness that weeping has an honored place in the life of faith. Why are Christians, of all people, embarrassed by tears, uneasy in the presence of sorrow, unpracticed in the language of lament? It certainly is not a biblical heritage, for virtually all our ancestors in the faith were thoroughly *'acquainted with grief.'* And our Savior was, as everyone knows, a *'Man of Sorrows.'*"[84]

In our lifelong pilgrimage to reflect more and more the image of Christ, perhaps we should remember what He did when His friend Lazarus died.

He wept.

"When Jesus saw her [Mary] weeping, and the Jews who had come along with her also weeping, he was deeply moved in spirit and troubled. 'Where have you laid him [Lazarus]?' he asked. 'Come and see, Lord,' they replied. Jesus wept. Then the Jews said, 'See how he loved him!'" (John 11:33-36).

This year our church enjoyed a Christmas concert by Michael Card, one of my all-time favorite musicians. I was thrilled to hear classic renditions of his "Immanuel" and "Joseph's Song." But the highlight for me was when he quietly shared with the audience the affirmation that many people are in pain and sorrow, especially during the holiday season. He then went on to relate some of his own journey of lament, which he so beautifully writes about in his book *A Sacred Sorrow*.

After introducing this song as the favorite of all he has written, Michael began to quietly sing "Come Lift Up Your Sorrows." In it, he urges us to allow the sorrow in our lives to be manifest with tears. His poignant words point out that there is great freedom to cry in the sacred place that Christ has provided. Being given permission to weep in the midst of the holiday season was actually the highlight of my evening.

The definition of lament is "to mourn aloud; to express sorrow or regret; cry out in grief; complain."

I can do that.

Even though instruction in lament seems to be have been left out of most Christian education programs and seminaries. The Bible, however, includes at least eighty psalms of lament.

If weeping was good enough for King David, it is most certainly good enough for me.

I once read a challenge from a pastor, "If I don't know what you are afraid of, I don't really know you." That changed my whole way of looking at relationships and authentic sharing.

I'd like to revise that statement and say, "If I don't know what causes you pain and how you *hurt*, then I don't really know you."

We are called to share our hurts and sorrows with one another.

"Our failure to lament cuts us off from each other. If you and I are to know one another in a deep way, we must not only share our hurts, anger, and disappointments with each other (which we often do), we must also lament them together before the God who hears and is moved by our tears. Only then does our sharing become truly redemptive in character. The degree to which I am willing to enter into the suffering of another person reveals the level of my commitment and love for them. If I am not interested in your hurts, I am not really interested in you."[85]

In the middle of writing this chapter today, I was compelled to take a break and "live these words." Two friends and I drove to a funeral home to hold and *weep* with our friend Susan, whose young daughter had just died. There were few words and no answers, just a quiet sense of our presence, our embrace, our entering into her pain, and sharing the lament for this young woman's life ended all too soon.

Who will you *weep* with today?

live these words

Everyone knows someone who is crying today. Who do you know facing grief, loneliness, despair, illness, or abandonment? Will you do something to reach out to them? If you can't literally show up and *weep with those who weep,* here are some other ideas: pray for them, make a phone call, mail a thinking-of-you card or postcard, drop off flowers from your garden (or market), or make arrangements to take over a "tea party in a basket"* and then visit over tea and treats (*tea party in a basket—keep packed for such occasions: two teacups/saucers, a small teapot, several bags of black and caffeine-free tea, dainty napkins, package of shortbread cookies/treats and small tray. All you have to do at your friend's house is heat water. Just be there and listen).

The Northumbria Community has some wonderful wisdom for those in grief. "Do not hurry as you walk with grief; it does not help the journey. Walk slowly, pausing often; do not hurry as you walk with grief. Be not disturbed by memories that come unbidden. Swiftly forgive; and let Christ speak for you unspoken words. Unfinished conversation will be resolved in Him. Be not disturbed. Be gentle with the one who walks with grief. If it is you, be gentle with yourself. Swiftly forgive; walk slowly, pausing often. Take time, be gentle as you walk with grief."[86]

pray these words

Dear Man of Sorrows, so acquainted with grief, Help me not to recoil from Your wounds, not to fear touching them or to be touched by them. Help me to understand that in my suffering I am not only nearest to You, but nearest to becoming like You. It's a sobering thought and I shudder when I think of it. Help me to understand that many of the sorrows I experience in this life belong to the nature of the world I live in, and will not pass away until this world passes away. Thank You for being in the midst of these sorrows, transforming them into blessings and filling them with meaning. Amen.

                           ঙ Ken Gire[87]

day 28

welcome

...WELCOME strangers into your home. By doing this,
some people have welcomed angels as guests,
without even knowing it. Hebrews 13:2 CEV

I'm not always at the fellowship coffee break between
church services.

I know I should be, but sometimes I have to get home
early, and sometimes I just feel overwhelmed with greeting
all those people. When you're in a large church with several
services, there are people who may be new faces to you, but
they have actually been around a long time. Know what I
mean? What if I welcomed a guest and they told me they
had been a member for years?

After all, I should know better. I am the wife of one
of their pastors.

However, one particular Sunday in late summer I was behind a fellowship hall table, helping to publicize an upcoming event, when I noticed a couple I'd never seen before. So I walked over to welcome them and discovered they had just arrived from Michigan and were visiting various churches in the area. We had a grand chat and before I knew it, I was getting Vickie's phone number and inviting her to a women's conference in two weeks.

And then before I knew it, I was inviting her to join my women's Bible study.

I certainly don't jump in like this with everyone I meet, but we seemed to immediately connect on a heart level, so I was thrilled when she showed up that Tuesday night. One of the gals I introduced her to was Lynn, a teacher at our church's nursery school. Vickie had just retired from teaching and offered to be a substitute if it was ever needed. Much to our surprise later that week the director of the nursery school took Vickie out to lunch and offered her a job that had unexpectedly just become available.

Such a grand serendipity.

I casually asked Vickie, the "Kiddie Lit" expert, to name her current favorite children's book. She said, *Pete the Cat—I Love My White Shoes.* What a fun story of Pete whose new white shoes get into all kinds of messy situations, but who chooses to respond with, "It's all good." She loaned me her copy to read, but I immediately told her I needed that book for a retreat I was speaking at soon so she gave it to me. If she thought it was odd that someone she just met would be so bold, she didn't flinch when she handed it over.

Such generosity.

A few weeks later our dear missionary friends from Bangladesh happened to be visiting on furlough. When I asked Jan about her vision for the orphaned street kids, she shared she was going to start a school in the park and needed simple materials to help teach the kids English.

I gave her Vickie's *Pete the Cat* book and now it is being used in Bangladesh to the delight of many, many children. Don't worry; I did eventually replace our copies with new *Pete the Cat* books as well as little Pete stuffed animals.

A few months later, Mike and I asked Bob and Vickie to join our couples Life Group and they have been a perfect fit with everyone. We love going to their home, and they have enjoyed ours as well. Sometimes you just meet people who feel like old friends. Our two daughters and their daughter all got married this year, and we had fun praying for each other through those events.

In fact, just before our weddings, Vickie and Bob offered to host our Dutch family members in their home the entire week of the wedding. What a blessing and answer to prayer for us, but also especially to our relatives who felt so well taken care of and loved by this couple.

I realize this story is not profound, nor unusual. But it is a great illustration of our word for the day—*welcome*.

When we extend a welcome to someone else, we have no idea how much it means to them, for sure. I realized this recently when Vickie shared how our meeting had been used to enrich her family's settling in process here in Connecticut.

But we especially have no idea how much it can eventually mean to us when we discover we have *welcomed angels as guests, without even knowing it.* Just today I found out that Vickie has been appointed the new director of our church's nursery school, upon our current director's retirement. All I can think is, *What if I hadn't reached out to that couple?* Of course, God has plenty of ways to bring His will about, but still.

Strangers become friends. Gifts get multiplied. Lives are enriched simply because we are willing to widen our circle.

So often people are wary of extending a welcome to their homes, worried that others will find their house messy, their décor tacky, their food tasteless, or their neighborhood humble. I call that being in bondage to C.H.A.O.S.—Can't Have Anyone Over Syndrome.

My advice? Get over yourself and ask someone in.

I assure you they won't do the white glove test for dust; they will simply be thrilled to have a homey evening with you.

The best times around our table feature meals of simple soup or stew and fresh bread and cheese. When we look at it as *entertaining,* we put all the focus on *ourselves* and the things we provide—the decorations, the food, the drink, the money spent. But when we view welcoming as *hospitality,* we put the focus on the *other person*—getting to know them, having fun, and making sure that they sense Jesus' presence among us all.

Yes, welcoming takes an effort. Sometimes we are rebuffed. Sometimes reaching out to others causes more complication than joy. But, in the long run, it's always worth it.

Remember, there might be *angels.*

live these words

So, here's your assignment. Try to do at least one of these: 1) Make an effort to meet someone new this week at work, school, church, or club. Introduce yourself and show interest in them, possibly asking them to accompany you somewhere in the days ahead. 2) Host (alone or with a friend) a gathering where you live. Plan simple food, or even ask folks to bring something. Before you invite anyone, pray and ask God to bring names to mind. Remember to keep things simple. In your invite, give a time span such as 'I'm having some folks over from 6:30 to around 9 for supper and the Yankees game/Scrabble/Downton Abbey/ making Christmas ornaments, etc. Do you want to join us?"

You can do it! Let me know if you meet any angels.

pray these words

Lord Jesus, You welcomed all who came into Your presence. May I reflect that same spirit through this ministry of hospitality. May Your light shine in my heart this day. Remove from me anything that would stand in the way of radiating Your presence. As people enter this Church to worship and praise You, may they hear Your voice in my words and see your love in my actions. May my "welcome" reflect our joy at their presence and my "good-bye" encourage them to return soon. I thank You for the opportunity to serve You and ask Your blessing upon all of my efforts. I ask this through our God who is the Giver of all gifts. Amen.

ଔ Minister of Hospitality Prayer[88]

day 29

remember

REMEMBER the days of old; consider
the generations long past. Ask your father and
he will tell you, your elders, and they will explain to you.
Deuteronomy 32:7

*N**o one tells a better story than Daddy*, I think, as I
snuggle under the covers and listen to him tell familiar
tales of his Depression-era childhood, of when he heard
Frank Sinatra at a college dance, or how he became a World
War II bomber pilot at age eighteen.

As he deftly segues from story to song, the lilting
tune of "I'll Be Seeing You" begins a set of old standards,
Daddy playing the piano by ear.

Listening from the next room, I smile, even as the
tears run down my cheeks. Daddy has been in heaven for

more than two years now—tonight his voice is coming from the CD player.

I'm staying on the sofa bed in Mama's assisted-living apartment. My parents were married for sixty-two years; my widowed mother chooses to fall asleep each night to the recorded strains of her beloved singing love songs.

To her.

Fortunately, we have many, many recordings of stories and songs by Daddy, the consummate storyteller. So it's not hard at all for me to *remember the days of old*.

Especially when I'm visiting my South Georgia hometown.

I *remember* sweet iced tea and fried cornbread every night for supper, paired with the best farm-to-table vegetables you can imagine—white acre peas, summer squash, and okra. Yes, okra. What I most remember is that our whole family gathered around the table for supper together every single night, catching up on the day's events.

I *remember* Mama sewing all our clothes and dressing her three daughters alike. However, I, being the middle one, was always given a contrasting color. For effect.

Things haven't changed much. I still wear color to stand out from the crowd.

I *remember* family prayers, our player piano, music, and laughter. Lots of laughter. Daddy recording our stories and poems and ramblings on his huge reel-to-reel tape player.

For posterity, of course, so that my much-more-mature self could listen in the present day...and *remember*.

What do you *remember* of days gone by and is it even important to do so? Why do you think God calls us to remember and *ask your fathers*?

Because life stories and spiritual milestones need to be passed along.

Tonight as I lie in Mama's den, the same disc also includes Daddy talking about attending a youth convention in Norway right after World War II. He speaks of the devastation all over Europe, witnessed by these young people who had gathered to promote peace and faith among the nations. Together with his extensive journals and poetry, we have a remarkable legacy of the life of my beloved father.

Often when I speak to groups and mention the importance of legacy I ask my audience if they remember at least one grandparent who touched their lives in a significant way. Almost everyone raises their hand. But then I say, "If you could spend one more day with that grandparent, what would you do?"

Invariably the answers are quite similar, "Listen to their stories. Ask lots of questions. Absorb their wisdom. Tell them how much I admire and appreciate who they are. Assure them of my love."

When we are younger, it seems that we have all the time in the world. And so we rarely make time to sit down and visit the past, hear of the stories of God's faithfulness in the lives of those who have lived and witnessed far more than ourselves. But God knows that we would be better prepared for today and the future if we learned from the past.

He entreats us to *ask our fathers and our elders*. Today there are some innovative organizations that are seeking to help record oral history from senior citizens. There are also teachers who routinely set up pairings between young people and seniors so they can get to know each other and share stories and wisdom. These are encouraging signs that we are perhaps turning back to the reverence for our elders.

God's chosen people also had a hard time *remembering*. Perhaps that's why periodically He would instruct them to establish stones of remembrance. One of my favorites occurs after Joshua led the Israelites across the Jordan River into the Promised Land and God instructed each priest from the twelve tribes to take a stone from the riverbed and place it on the shore as a remembrance of what happened that day, calling it Gilgal.

> In the future when your descendants ask their parents, "What do these stones mean?" tell them, "Israel crossed the Jordan on dry ground." For the LORD your God dried up the Jordan before you until you had crossed over…He did this so that all the peoples of the earth might know that the hand of the LORD is powerful and so that you might always fear the LORD your God (Joshua 4:21-24).

Samuel, an Old Testament prophet, priest, and judge over Israel, also erected a stone of remembrance and called it Ebenezer, which means "stone of help." In his lifetime there had been twenty years of sorrow in Israel (because of disobedience and idol worship), and Samuel had boldly told the people that if they were truly sorry, they should do something about it and get rid of their idols. So the people gathered at Mizpah to fight the Philistines. At Samuel's instruction, they poured water on the ground before the Lord as a sign of repentance for sin, turning from idols, and indicating a decision to obey God once more.

God ushered them into victory, and as a result of this significant event, "Then Samuel took a stone and set it upright between Mizpah and Shen. He named it Ebenezer, explaining, saying 'Thus far the LORD has helped us'" (1 Samuel 7:12).

Yet another stone of remembrance occurred in the life of Jacob after he deceived his father, Isaac, and stole his brother Esau's blessing. Fleeing for his life, he found only a stone for a pillow. While sleeping in the wilderness, he dreamed of a ladder going up to heaven, with angels ascending and descending it, declaring God's promise, "I am with you and will watch over you wherever you go, and I will bring you back to this land. I will not leave you until I have done what I promised you" (Genesis 28:15).

With this new promise, Jacob changed his stone pillow into a stone of remembrance by pouring oil on it and naming it Bethel, which means "house of God." Then he made a pledge to God that because God had blessed him, he would always follow God.

Those who lived before us helped shape who we are today, and we can honor them by *remembering* all they experienced and taught us. Perhaps your own loved ones won't have a monument erected in their memory, but you can always fashion your own "stones of remembrance" from the lives they lived.

Let us join the psalmist, "We will...tell to the coming generation the glorious deeds of the LORD, and his might, and the wonders that he has done...he commanded our fathers to teach their children, that the next generation might know them, the children yet unborn, and arise to tell them to their children...." (Psalm 78:4-6 ESV).

May we learn from our fathers and mothers the most important lesson of all.

To *remember*.

live these words

What can you do to pass along your own life stories? Why not make a video, recording you telling stories and sharing life lessons for future generations? Think how much fun your own children will have showing this to your future grandchildren one day. It will be a treasure worth more than money.

With easily accessible digital publishing, anyone can write their own book of stories or family history or original poetry. There are also many great outlets for spiritual scrapbooking, both online, and creatively on paper.

Tell the stories of your childhood, what made you laugh, what frightened you, a turning point, a decision that changed your life, your favorite teacher and why, your first heartbreak, your first job, interesting people you met along the way and what they taught you. There are endless bits and pieces of our lives that will pass along encouragement and strength to a future generation. The hardest part of this exercise is that the young people may not at all be interested in them now. So when you write or film, remember, "We must all plant a few trees we will never get to sit under."

Another idea that I share in my book *Role of a Lifetime* is the Seasons of Life calendar where each month represents seven years of our lives. It is a great exercise to jot down memories and significant events from each month and season. Write these down for your own review and for future generations.

Looking back is not simply reminiscing, it is looking back to become aware of new possibilities.

January/ ages 0-7 …

February/ ages 8-14 …

March/ ages 15-21 …

April/ ages 22-28 …

May/ ages 29-35 …

June/ ages 36-42 …

July/ ages 43-49 …

August/ ages 50-56 …

September/ ages 57-63 …

October/ ages 64-70 …

November/ ages 71-77…

December/ ages 78-100 …

pray these words

O Lord, give me the wisdom of spiritual remembrance so that I will never take the riches of Your grace and goodness for granted. Remind me to recall all of Your many benefits and blessings over the years and to realize frequently how much You have done for me. You have carried me through difficult passages. You have comforted me in times of despair. You have encouraged me when I was despondent. You have given me hope when all seemed lost. You have blessed me with freedoms, friends and opportunities that I never deserved. As I review Your benefits in the past, let me also reflect on Your process in my present and on Your prospects for my future. In light of all this, I can fully affirm that Your will for me is good and acceptable and perfect. May this gratitude of remembrance give me perspective and peace in the present moment. Amen.

ဢ Kenneth Boa[89]

day 30

LOOK to the Lord and His strength; seek His face always.
1 Chronicles 16:11

She was lovely. Not only that, her life of privilege, art, and leisure in London was promising and full. Art critic John Ruskin enthusiastically proclaimed her to be one of the best artists of the nineteenth century.

But it wasn't enough.

Lilias Trotter's devotion to Christ compelled her to abandon that world for an entirely different life in North Africa. There her love of literature and art became dynamic tools for evangelism, and her compassionate lifestyle of love and encouragement captured the hearts of the Muslim people.

Her struggle (and eventual victory) in the whole area of finding focus inspired Helen Lemmel to write this hymn in 1922: *Turn your eyes upon Jesus, Look full in His wonderful face, And the things of earth will grow strangely dim, In the light of His glory and grace.*[90]

Our verse today urges us to *look* to the Lord. To *seek His face always.* To focus only on Him.

Easy to say, hard to do. Especially in our world of endless distractions.

And yet, even Lilias fought hard for focus back in her day. "Never has it been so easy to live in half a dozen good harmless worlds at once—art, music, social science, games, motoring, the following of some profession, and so on. And between them we run the risk of drifting about, the 'good' hiding the 'best.'"[91]

While her life in London was good, Lilias decided to respond to God by actively looking for the best. She eventually found it in Algeria where she extended Christ's love and care to Muslims for forty years, despite great odds, her own Algerian Mission Band eventually grew into an international work now known as Pioneers.

I, too, often have trouble distinguishing between the good and the best simply because there are so many choices these days. Life is like a kaleidoscope—one of those optical toys in a tube that produce many different colors and patterns as bits of colored glass are reflected by mirrors. The more you twist the kaleidoscope, the more variations of glass appear. No wonder the definition of the word has come to mean "a complex set of events or circumstances."

That certainly describes my own life today. There is so much that shimmers and shines and changes and confuses. Every time we blink, another image is flashed upon the screen of our minds, not to mention the screens of our computers, cell phones, and iPads. No wonder we are distracted with a kind of kaleidoscope living.

The word "distraction" comes from the Latin *distractus,* which literally means "to draw or pull apart." In his book *The Attentive Life*, Leighton Ford says, "It can have a very innocuous sense: a distraction can be an amusement or diversion that relaxes us. But more seriously a distraction is a pull away from what deep down we know is our most fundamental goal, purpose or direction. When we are distracted, we are often confused by conflicting emotions or worries. The more 'noise' that surrounds us, the more we absorb, the more likely we are to be distractible, our attention readily diverted and restless, and the more vulnerable we become to all the distractions around."[92]

And sometimes miss seeing God.

I occasionally find myself multi-tasking, only to discover I haven't really given my undivided attention to any one thing. I easily get sidetracked by all the choices out there, whether technological (web surfing or social networking) or sensory (at the mall or giant food store). Sometimes I reach day's end only to find that, though quite busy, I missed important encounters and opportunities because I was always looking beyond...to the next thing.

Ours is a world of "continuous partial attention," an apt description by one Microsoft researcher of our current overload living. Because we are expected to be "on" 24/7, no one person or thing ever gets our full focus, sometimes not even God.

The psalmist reminds us to "Keep your eyes open for God, watch for his works; be alert for signs of his presence" (Psalm 105:4 THE MESSAGE).

When my children were younger, we would go around the supper table and share our God-sightings of the day—

times where He clearly showed up. Even now, I smile when an adult child calls from across the country and speaks of an incident that was such a "God-thing."

Look for Him every moment. There are so many "God-things" out there for each one of us to see.

live these words

If you find it hard to look for God and focus on Him alone, perhaps this prayer by the psalmist will help: "Turn my eyes from looking at what is worthless; give me life in Your ways" (Psalm 119:37 HCSB). What are the "worthless" things clamoring for your focus? Often in driver's education class students are taught that focusing their attention on oncoming headlights might cause them to drift into the wrong lane. This tendency holds true in many other aspects of life—we will be drawn to whatever gains our attention.

Take some time and reflect on what you are most readily drawn to, and through prayer, ask God if you need to turn from that and give more attention to Him.

How can you determine whether or not you are "continually partially attentive" without being fully focused on anything? Well, have you finished reading one whole book lately? When did you last sit down for a period of time and look into your child or friend or spouse's eyes and really listen to what they had to say? What scripture penetrated your heart this week from your devotions or worship or class—do you even remember it? Perhaps your answers to these questions will help you understand where you need to begin. Be intentional and remember to "keep your eyes open for God, watch for His works."

pray these words

I pray that the eyes of my heart may be enlightened so I may know what is the hope of His calling, what are the glorious riches of His inheritance among the saints, and what is the immeasurable greatness of His power to us who believe, according to the working of His vast strength" (praying Ephesians 1:18-19).

O Lord my God, teach my heart this day where and how to see You, where and how to find You. You have made me and remade me, and You have bestowed on me all the good things I possess, and still I do not know You. I have not yet done that for which I was made. Teach me to seek You, for I cannot seek You unless You teach me, or find You unless You show Yourself to me. Let me seek You in my desire, let me desire You in my seeking. Let me find You by loving You, let me love You when I find You. Amen.

                     ಬ Anselm (1033-1109)[93]

day 31

choose

...CHOOSE life, so that you and your children may live
and that you may love the Lord Your God, listen to His
voice, and hold fast to Him. Deuteronomy 30:19-20

*M*y child is now having a child. She is *choosing life*—
to become a mother.

And I can't help but remember the day I walked
out of a Seattle courtroom as her adoptive mother. I have
learned so much since choosing her. I hope.

Parenting is a choice not to be taken lightly. It is a
privilege, an honor, and a lifelong commitment. Because
we are not only life-givers when the child is born, but every
subsequent choice we make either gives life to them or
takes a piece of it away.

Our heavenly Father knows all about hard choices.

In the book of Deuteronomy, the Hebrews had turned away from God and He knew that in the future, they would inevitably make more bad choices. Yet He still offered them words to live: "They are not just idle words for you—they are your life." (Deuteronomy 32:47).

The people of Israel had wandered from God during their long desert sojourn, but Moses is pleading with them to return, assuring that God will take them back and offer inward spiritual renewal (circumcised hearts, Deuteronomy 30:6). He reminds them, "...this command...is not too hard for you; it is not beyond what you can do" (Deuteronomy 30:11 NCV).

Do you sometimes feel that what God is calling you to is actually too difficult? Practically impossible? This verse reminds us that God will always provide what is needed to do what He requires.

And what are they being asked to do? "...love the Lord, your God; to walk in obedience to Him, and to keep His commands, decrees and laws; then you will live and increase, and the LORD your God will bless you in the land you are entering to possess" (Deuteronomy 30:16).

Love Him. Follow Him. Obey Him. And the reward? That our children might also live a life full and close to the living God.

Who wouldn't want that for their children?

And yet, even the best parent falters and fails. I know I have.

I entered motherhood with great desire and determination to pour love and courage and joy and hope into the boys and girls God entrusted me with for such a short time. And I meant it. And I tried to do it. With a full measure of grace and mercy.

But, unfortunately, not all the time.

Sometimes I made different choices—choosing self over others; choosing temper over temperance; choosing control over release; choosing fear over trust; choosing loud over quiet; choosing lethargy over an active response to God's words.

As another kindred spirit parent prayed, "The list of things I wrongly choose could go on and on. And sometimes I act on these things in ways that are darker than I even care to state. Each time I make such a choice, I choose death (Romans 6:23). Today, I ask that You would breathe life into my soul afresh and enable me to choose life—to choose You and Your ways."[94]

In our text, the two choices set before the people were "life or death; blessings or curses" (Deuteronomy 30:19). When we choose life and blessings for ourselves, the benefits spill over to our children.

I believe that grace-filled parenting is the healthiest way to raise kids. Researchers say that all people of every culture share the same three inner needs: 1. Secure love; 2. Significant purpose; 3. Strong hope.

The same is true for the children entrusted to our care. We need to provide an atmosphere that *promotes security*—assuring them they are accepted and loved, no matter what; *offers significance*—helping them understand their unique gifts and leanings and then urging them to courageously pursue all God has for them; and *provides strength*—cultivating inner fortitude to keep going in difficult times and placing their hope in God.

Somehow we must allow our children to learn the hard way, even to fail. They need to know that God (and we) offers second chances. That actions have consequences and that choices do make a difference. If we focus more on trying to please others than on pleasing God, our children will get the message that they must earn our favor and others' approval. Instead, we should encourage them to rest securely in the unconditional love of Christ and to find purpose in glorifying Him in all they do.

That's why our choices matter.

Every choice we make lifts up a character value to those so closely watching our lives. When we exhibit honor and courtesy to older adults, we are showing that we value their lives and wisdom far beyond our own. When a young dad takes the family to worship service and records the game instead, he is showing that he may love football, but he loves God more. The way we handle money and conflict and relatives and holidays and politics and work pressure and friendships speaks loudly to the next generation.

May our choices always bring life to those around us.

For now.

And for the future we will never see.

live these words

Our word and text today are for everyone, even though I chose to illustrate it through the eyes of a parent. But whether or not you are a parent, the important thing to remember is that choices in life matter. Not just to us, but to those caught in an ever-widening ripple effect. So think of a choice you made recently. Write it down. Now expand the parameters of influence through that choice. How did it affect you and thus those you love—for better and for worse? What about the things/people you had to say "no" to because you said "yes"? Begin to explore the wisdom of this entire verse, which emphasizes that our ultimate goal is to make choices that result in greater love and obedience to God.

pray these words

Father, hear us, we are praying. Hear the words our hearts are saying. We are praying for our children. Keep them from the powers of evil, from the secret hidden peril, from the whirlpool that would suck them, from the treacherous quicksand, pluck them. From the worldling's hollow gladness, from the sting of faithless sadness, Holy Father, save our children. Through life's troubled waters steer them, through life's bitter battle cheer them, Father, Father, be Thou near them. Read the language of our longing, read the wordless pleadings thronging, Holy Father, for our children. And wherever they may bide, lead them home at eventide. Amen.

                                    ஐ Amy Carmichael (1867-1951)[95]

day 32

LEAVE all your worries with Him, because
He cares for you. 1 Peter 5:7 GNT

*W*hen I arrived home from the conference Sunday
evening, I realized a hitchhiker had accompanied me
in the door.

His name was Worry.

At once he set to work bringing up all those things
that had conveniently been dormant while I had focused
on an enjoyable weekend of ministry. One by one, people
and circumstances—what ifs and if onlys—popped into my
mind and got me to thinking.

And worrying.

I might as well have snatched back from God
everything (and everyone) I had ever entrusted to Him. I

might as well have emailed all those women to just forget what I had taught them, because by now even I wasn't buying it.

I had retrieved those worries and was planning to carry them—drag them—along into my new week. Oh yeah, that hitchhiker had already settled in to my home and heart quite comfortably.

My grandmother used to say, "Worry is a lot like a rocking chair. It gives you something to do, but you don't get anywhere."

Actually worry causes *re*gress, not *pro*gress. Experts say that most of what we spend time worrying about never actually comes to pass. Think of all that time and energy spent worrying, now lost to us forever.

I, for one, do not have any time or energy to waste that way.

I'm also not prepared to pay the price of holding on to my worries. "Just from a medical perspective, living in a constant state of anxiety, worry, or fear can cause all kinds of irritability and frustration, mood swings, depression, and decreased mental function…. Worry can lead to a lot of loss. Loss of memory, loss of perspective, loss of rationality, loss of ability to concentrate, loss of ability to think clearly, prioritize, and make wise decisions. Loss of ability to differentiate facts from feelings. In the Old Testament, confusion was a weapon God often used to destroy the wicked. It's not what He wants for His beloved children" (1 Corinthians 14:33).[96]

What a good incentive to do what our text today says, *Leave all your worries with Him*. Why would you do that? *Because He cares for you.*

God wants to carry our burdens. God wants to assure us that He has everything under control and we can leave all concerns in His care. As one medical doctor observes, "God is not pacing the throne room anxious and depressed because of the condition of the world. He knows, He is not surprised, and He is sovereign."[97]

Hannah Whitall Smith, author of the classic nineteenth-century book *Christian's Secret of a Happy Life*, actually lived anything but a happy life. Her husband was a famous preacher who secretly struggled with alcohol and not so secretly had numerous adulterous affairs. Of her seven children, four died young, one daughter abandoned her own children, another married famous atheist Bertrand Russell, and her youngest son rejected Christianity.

I would guess Hannah had plenty to worry about, yet she still wrote these words, embraced by many in their own difficult times. "The circumstances of her life she could not alter, but she took them to the Lord, and handed them over into His management; and then she believed that He took it, and she left all the responsibility and the worry and anxiety with Him. She abandoned her whole self to the Lord, with all that she was and all that she had; and, believing that He took that which she had committed to Him, she ceased fret and worry."[98]

Some of us excuse our worrying by saying that it's just our nature to do so. Nothing could be farther from the truth—we make a choice to worry.

Not only that, the root words for "worry" are rather violent. The Old English derivation is *wyrgan*, which means "to strangle." This term later evolved into *worien,* which meant "grabbing another creature by the throat with your teeth and shaking it to death." Okay.

Author and radio teacher Christin Ditchfield explains, "When we worry, that's what we do. We deliberately ignore

God's admonishment to take every thought captive (2 Corinthians 10:5), not be anxious and trust Him. Instead, we latch on to a bunch of negative thoughts. We grab them with our teeth and refuse to let go of them. We churn. We toss and turn. We shake them this way and that. From a distance it looks like we're strangling them. But the truth is, they're strangling us."[99]

Kick that hitchhiker out of your heart and home.

Instead, draw near to the One who cares for you and me. *Leave* every person, every circumstance, every concern at the foot of the Cross.

live these words

When worry threatens to take over your life, remember this sixteenth-century quote from Teresa of Avila. "Let nothing disturb you. Let nothing frighten you. All things are passing away:. God never changes. Patience obtains all things. Whoever has God lacks nothing. God alone suffices."[100]

On Good Friday, each one who comes to our afternoon church service receives a small slip of paper upon arrival. During the meditation, we are encouraged to write down all the situations and people that we are carrying with great concern. At the end of the Good Friday vigil, our ancient bell in the tower tolls thirty-three times at exactly three o'clock (the years in Jesus' earthly life and the time of his death). We then solemnly proceed to a large wooden cross on the chancel for the service and impale our tiny folder paper on one of the many nails. Then, our four pastors gently take each paper from the cross, placing them in baskets. In complete silence we follow as they stand outside on the patio, burning each and every page, representative of all our burdens. We left them at the foot of the cross. We no longer carry them. This symbolic exercise is what it truly means to *leave* all your worries with Him.

pray these words

Father, thank you for providing for my every need. Thank you that I don't have to spend my days consumed with worry; I can be consumed with You. No need enters my life for which you have not already planned and provided. I choose to keep anxiety from cluttering my heart, and instead let it be filled with You. Amen.

                     ɞ Jennifer Kennedy Dean[101]

day 33

shine

...*SHINE* like stars in the dark world.
Philippians 2:15 NCV

*H*ere at "Sunnyside" cottage, our New England winter darkness descends each day at 4:30, so that's when the clear lights on our screen porch Christmas tree appear. And, if I'm home, I run around to light the candoliers in each of our windows. We are eager to *shine* some brightness into our lives, our neighborhood, our world.

Anything to dispel the encroaching darkness.

On the first Sunday of Advent the scripture both sung and read is from Isaiah 9:2, "The people walking in darkness have seen a great light; on those living in the land of deep darkness a light has dawned."

Seems like a good way to describe our current culture —"people walking in darkness."

Even as that baby Jesus arrived to a people who had been waiting in darkness for a very long time—400 years of hoping for some light to *shine*—just so He comes to us today, to our increasingly dark world.

During the past holiday season, my little state of Connecticut marked the one-year anniversary of unspeakable horror—the Sandy Hook school killings of twenty-six innocent children and educators. Two of my author/speaker friends recently lost their battle with cancer, while another is mourning the unexpected death of her young son. Closer to home, a new friend has relapsed and is in recovery treatment in an institution for the entire holidays. Friends are losing jobs, homes, and hope.

Honestly, you know I could go on and on...sadly, there are endless stories of darkness.

Into all this, Christmas still comes. Every year.

Christ comes—the Light.

Whether or not we are ready. Whether or not it is convenient. As fellow Connecticut author Madeleine L'Engle wrote in her poem "First Coming,"

> He did not wait till hearts were pure.
> In joy He came
> To a tarnished world of sin and doubt.
> To a world like ours, of anguished shame
> He came, and his Light would not go out.[102]

Those of us who have had experience with the lure of darkness, the prison of darkness, the secret of darkness —are the very ones who should choose to *shine* that light into the dark corners around us. In our verse today Paul compares us to the brightness of stars.

I recently read a news article that reported a new startling statistic. There are three times more stars in the universe than we originally thought. Scientists have confirmed 300 sextillion stars. In case you can't wrap your head around that number, let me break it down for you — three trillion times one hundred billion.

That's a lot of stars.

When I read this news report I remembered, "He [God] determines the number of the stars and calls them each by name" (Psalm 147:4). As I was further pondering, I came across a quote from esteemed Harvard astrophysicist Charlie Conroy, "So the number of stars in the universe is equal to all the cells in the humans on Earth—a kind of funny coincidence."[103]

Far be it for me to challenge a Harvard astrophysicist, but, excuse me, there are no coincidences with God the Creator of the universe! He promised to make "descendents as numerous as the stars in the sky...all nations on earth will be blessed..." (Genesis 26:4).

I may only be one of 300 sextillion, but God knows my name—and yours. And He calls me to *shine like stars the dark world*.

God shines on us. We, then, *shine* on those in our world.

So I am doing my part. To *shine*. Not just because I love wearing sequins and bling (though I do, when the occasion calls for it), but because I know that everywhere I go, there is someone who needs a bit more light, hope, and encouragement.

And I plan to live up to my name (Lucinda is derived from the Latin word for light).

We *shine* because the light comes from Christ within us. Author Frederica Mathewes-Green explains it this way, "God is Light, and we are filled with His light—maybe even literally, as some saints were said to visibly glow. The term for this transformation is fairly scandalizing: *theosis,* which means 'being transformed into God'.... Of course we do not become little mini-gods with our own universes. We never lose our identity, but we are filled with God like a sponge is filled with water."[104]

What dark places will you light up today?

live these words

Halloween is my least favorite holiday, but I can appreciate jack-o-lanterns, especially now that people are creatively making the faces funny rather than frightening. The concept is to put a bright candle inside a scooped out pumpkin. Then, the carved holes become the openings for the light to shine through. I believe that's how God wants us to *shine*—from the inside out. Which means that there must be something bright inside to begin with (inner soul work, folks).

But it also means that holes are necessary. Those gaps and mistakes. Those limps and losses. They can be opportunities for us to be real with one another. To show that although we have been broken and bruised at times, we still *shine* brightly into the darkness.

The world is watching. The darkness threatens. But we can reflect the true Light; we can *shine!*

pray these words

Dear Jesus, Help us to spread Your fragrance everywhere we go. Flood our souls with Your spirit and life. Penetrate and possess our whole being so utterly that our lives may only be a radiance of Yours. Shine through us and be so in us that every soul we come in contact with may feel Your presence in our soul. Let them look up and see no longer us but only Jesus. Stay with us and then we shall begin to shine as You shine, so to shine as to be light to others. The light, O Jesus, will be all from You. None of it will be ours. It will be You shining on others through us. Let us preach You without preaching, not by words but by our example, by the catching force, the sympathetic influence of what we do. The evident fullness of the love our heart bears to You. Amen.*

ᔍ John Henry Newman (1801-1890)[105]

*Today's prayer: prayed daily by Mother Teresa and the workers at her charity.

day 34

consider

...*CONSIDER* others as more important than
yourselves. Everyone should look out not only for
his own interests, but also for the interests of others.
Philippians 2:3-4 HCSB

*P*eople came from many nations and backgrounds to
the Lausanne Committee 1980 Consultation on World
Evangelization, held at a beachside resort in Pattaya,
Thailand. I was the communications editor for the event,
and my exposure to these servants of God from so many
different countries changed my worldview immensely.

But it was a simple story of two Americans that
fleshed out today's verse in a very real way.

Our venue was on the Gulf of Siam and rooms on one
side of the hotel had a magnificent view of the ocean, while

rooms across the hall saw only the ugly parking lot and dump outside their window. Boston area pastor Gordon MacDonald and seminary professor J. Christy Wilson arrived late at night and had gone straight to their shared room after a long travel day.

Gordon awoke early, opened the drapes, and looked out upon the dump, blurting out, "Oh, no, we got the terrible view."

Dr. Wilson, just awakening, immediately responded, "Isn't that wonderful! It means that some of the brothers and sisters from the Third World who have so little will get a chance to enjoy a beautiful sight this morning."

Gordon later commented on this gentle rebuke, "Almost *never* do I forget Dr. Wilson's words and his attitude when I feel the temptation to complain about something that does not seem in alignment with *my* best interests."[106]

Let's face it. Most of us do not automatically respond with such gestures of selfless consideration. And yet, we could. The assumption of others as better than ourselves could be our default reaction, rather than our try-hard reaction.

But only as we have the mind of Christ.

The apostle Paul admitted that this mindset was a struggle for him to achieve as well. Earlier in this passage he asks God to let him do nothing out of *selfish ambition* (translated from the Greek word *epithelia,* which means "jockeying for position or acclaim") or *vain conceit* (translated from the Greek word *kenodoxia* which means "empty praise or jealousy"). He then urges us all to *consider others* in advance of our own concerns.

That's exactly the way Dr. Wilson lived, and thus the first words out of his mouth that early morning (when he was barely awake) were joy that someone else would get the best view.

I am reminded of the hymn "May the Mind of Christ My Savior," based on this passage from Philippians 2:

> May the mind of Christ, my Savior,
> Live in me from day to day,
> By His love and power controlling
> All I do and say.
> May the love of Jesus fill me
> As the waters fill the sea;
> Him exalting, self-abasing,
> This is victory.
> May His beauty rest upon me,
> As I seek the lost to win,
> And may they forget the channel,
> Seeing only Him. [107]

These words embody a person of humility. One who seeks another's best before their own. One who is not only willing but also eager to have another shine brighter.

Do you want to be that kind of person?

"The way to Christ is first through *humility*, second through *humility*, third through *humility*," wrote Augustine in the fifth century. "If humility does not precede and accompany and follow every good work we do, if it is not before us to focus on, if it is not beside us to lean upon, if it is not behind us to fence us in, pride will wrench from our hand any good deed we do at the very moment we do it."[108]

I want to be that kind of person.

And so, one night at my women's Bible study on the Beatitudes, I blurted out, "I wish people thought of me as meek and humble!"

Everyone laughed.

It seems their collective association with the words "meek" and "humble" did not immediately conjure up my face. Not only that, but most people think of meek as weak or withdrawn or some other characteristic quite alien to a twenty-first-century Type A woman like myself.

But perhaps most people are wrong.

I still want to be meek and humble.

And this desire is quite natural for anyone seeking to live like Jesus who "humbled himself" (Philippians 2:8) in order to serve others. Even our Lord's words in Matthew 11:29 use the same root word as meek when He says, "...I am gentle and humble in heart...."

Why wouldn't I want to pursue this quality even though everything in my own nature goes against it?

Choosing to follow Christ on this path of considering others first is actually a sign of strength, not weakness, according to one Bible teacher, "The meek do not trust in their own ability nor do they act in their own strength. The Lord knows that it often appears that the loud, brash and overbearing inherit the land. But it is not really so. It sometimes looks like those who trust in themselves win the day.... The meek have the strength to wait it out and to let God work."[109]

Unfortunately, we have had more than two thousand years to absorb these words into our culture, tweak them a bit to our own liking, and then just carry on in a half-hearted way of humility when it's convenient but assertiveness when it's absolutely necessary.

I know. I do it, too.

Perhaps it would be helpful to review what the first generation of Christ-followers did in response to words that many of them actually heard Jesus say in person. A document from the philosopher Aristides in A.D. 125 described them this way:

> They walk in all humility and kindness, and falsehood is not found among them, and they love one another. They despise not the widow, and grieve not the orphan. He that has, distributes liberally to him who has not. If they see a stranger, they bring him under their roof, and rejoice over him as if he were their own brother: for they call themselves brethren, not after the flesh, but after the Spirit of God; but when one of their poor passes away from the world, and any of them see him, then he provides for his burial according to his ability; and if they hear that any of their number is imprisoned or oppressed for the name of their Messiah, all of them provide for his needs, and if it is possible that he may be delivered, they deliver him. And if there is among them a person that is poor and needy, and they have not an abundance of necessaries, they fast two or three days that they may supply the needy with their necessary food."[110]

If we are to live the words found in Philippians 2, we must obviously look after our own interests, which is not usually much of a stretch. But our primary focus should be first and always to look after the interests of others, *considering* them more important, more worthy.

Christ did that for you and me.
May we follow Him and do likewise.

live these words

Most of us are not wired for humility. Our default is usually self. But we can grow into a person who one day turns around and discovers that her first response was other-centered. This is called sanctification—becoming more and more like Jesus. And it won't be fully realized in us this side of heaven. However, we embody this verse every time we choose to lift others up, recognizing their value and their achievements. Or when we perhaps recommend them for a job or honor we would also like to have. We can truly practice being second place. The world won't understand because of the belief that self-promotion is essential to success.

But we will know. And God will know.

pray these words

O Jesus! meek and humble of heart, hear me.
From the desire of being esteemed,
deliver me, O Jesus.
From the desire of being loved,
deliver me, O Jesus.
From the desire of being extolled,
deliver me, O Jesus.

From the desire of being honored,
deliver me, O Jesus.
From the desire of being praised,
deliver me, O Jesus.
From the desire of being preferred to others,
deliver me, O Jesus.
From the desire of being consulted,
deliver me, O Jesus.
From the desire of being approved,
deliver me, O Jesus.
From the fear of being humiliated,
deliver me, O Jesus.
From the fear of being despised,
deliver me, O Jesus.
From the fear of suffering rebukes,
deliver me, O Jesus.
From the fear of being forgotten,
deliver me, O Jesus.
From the fear of being ridiculed,
deliver me, O Jesus.
From the fear of being wronged,
deliver me, O Jesus.
From the fear of being suspected,
deliver me, O Jesus.
That others may be loved more than I,
O Jesus, grant me the grace to desire it.
That others may be esteemed more than I,
O Jesus, grant me the grace to desire it.
That, in the opinion of the world, others may increase and I may decrease,
O Jesus, grant me the grace to desire it.

That others may be chosen and I set aside,
O Jesus, grant me the grace to desire it.
That others may be praised and I unnoticed,
O Jesus, grant me the grace to desire it.

That others may be preferred to me in everything,
O Jesus, grant me the grace to desire it.

That others may become holier than I, provided
that I may become as holy as I should,

O Jesus, grant me the grace to desire it. Amen.

    ❧ Cardinal Merry de Val (1865-1930)[111]

day 35

imprint

IMPRINT these words of Mine on your hearts and minds, bind them as a sign on your hands, and let them be a symbol on your foreheads. Teach them to your children, talking about them when you sit in your house and when you walk along the road, when you lie down and when you get up. Deuteronomy 11:18-19 HCSB

*A*s my eyes open after a long night of sleep, they slowly begin to focus on what's in front of me. Letters merge into words and I read them yet again—"Each day is a gift from God."

Three years ago when we moved into this 1940 cottage, I imprinted these words (a decal) on the slanted eaves of our bedroom wall, exactly at eye level, so that they would be the first words I saw when I woke up and the last words as I went to bed.

They are now deeply engrained in my mind and heart, prompting gratitude for the gift of life.

Our scripture today comes from Moses' warning to the people who have wandered in the desert for forty years and are soon to be crossing over into the Promised Land. He knows how easy it will be for them to, yet again, forget the faithfulness of the true God, and chase after other false gods. Perhaps that's why he suggests several ways to keep God's law in their lives—"imprint them," "tie them," "bind them," and "teach them."

Anything to make sure they don't forget the truth. They are encouraged to choose blessings over curses, life over death.

Today it is easy for our minds to get saturated with many other cultural messages. How can we, too, keep God's Word at the forefront?

One way is to memorize Scripture.

As a child, my first Scripture memory exercise was all of Psalm 23, and I assure you I can recite it perfectly to this day—ahh, the strength of a young brain. I also remember memorizing John 14 in my teens, a season when it was comforting for me to hear over and over again, "Let not your heart be troubled...."

As a college freshman, I claimed my life verse as Isaiah 58:10-11 and have recited it almost daily since then, to remind me both of what God wants me to do for Him and what He will keep doing for me. "If you spend yourselves in behalf of the hungry and satisfy the needs of the oppressed, then your light will rise in the darkness, and your night will become like the noonday. The Lord will guide you always; He will satisfy your needs in a sun-scorched land and will strengthen your frame. You will be like a well-watered garden, like a spring whose waters never fail."

And that was just my beginning. I have spent my adult life studying God's Word and committing portions of it to memory, sometimes intentionally, sometimes simply through repetition. This makes it so helpful to have a word when most needed—either for myself or to share with someone else.

The Bible studies I write for First Place 4 Health all include scripture memory cards, one verse for each week's study, as well as a CD with the memory verses set to music. Let's face it, if our minds easily memorize commercial jingles, how much better to sing Bible verses.

Author Chuck Swindoll heartily recommends such a practice. "I know of no other single practice in the Christian life more rewarding, practically speaking, than memorizing scripture…. No other single exercise pays greater spiritual dividends! Your prayer life will be strengthened. Your witnessing will be sharper, much more effective. Your counseling will be in demand. Your attitudes and outlook will begin to change. Your mind will become alert and observant. Your confidence and assurance will be enhanced. Your faith will be solidified."[112]

God's words bring life and light to us on the journey. This is greatly illustrated in C. S. Lewis' *The Silver Chair*. The Christ figure, Aslan the lion, tells Jill four signs to lead her on her journey and emphasizes their importance, "But, first, remember, remember, remember the signs. Say them to yourself when you wake in the morning and when you lie down at night, and when you wake in the middle of the night. And whatever strange things may happen to you, let nothing turn your mind from following the signs.

"Here on the mountain, the air is clear and your mind is clear; as you drop down into Narnia, the air will thicken. Take great care that it does not confuse your mind. And the signs, which you have learned here, will not look at all as you expect them to look, when you meet them there. That is why it is so important to know them by heart and pay no attention to appearances. Remember the signs and believe the signs. Nothing else matters."[113]

Jill leaves on her quest to find a lost prince, but along the way the signs are forgotten or misunderstood. Dire consequences ensue—the group begins without official support, they end up almost eaten by giants, and then fail to recognize the prince when they finally come face to face with him. The problem is that even though Jill has learned the signs, she cannot remember them.

When we are alone with God and in His Word, Scripture seems so clear, so life-giving. But then the atmosphere changes in our world and we get confused. Our distractions and fears cause us to forget even the most simple of commands such as, "Love the Lord your God with all your heart and with all your soul and with all your strength and with all your mind; and, love your neighbor as yourself" (Luke 10:27).

It's far too easy to veer from our desired course. That's why we need to learn to *imprint* the words on our hearts and minds. Let us remember every morning and every night and repeat them when we awaken in the middle of the night.

Only when we keep Christ fixed in our sight are we able to complete the journey and reach the destination God has for us.

live these words

How do you best upload God's Word into your heart and mind? Are you an auditory learner? Then say the verse aloud or listen to a version of the Bible while you walk, drive, or clean house. Are you a visual learner? Use a highlighter when you read, write passages in your journal, or print up scripture memory cards to keep in prominent view for easy recall. Are you an experiential learner? Then think of a way to use the story of the text in your life and associate it with something you do. But most of all stay in God's Word, seeking to understand the meaning and the implications for your life today.

pray these words

> *Most gracious God, our heavenly Father, in Whom alone dwells all the fullness of light and wisdom, enlighten our minds by Your Holy Spirit to truly understand Your Word. Give us grace to receive it reverently and humbly. May it lead us to put our whole trust in You alone, and so to serve and honour You that we may glorify Your holy name and encourage others by setting a good example. Amen.*

> ⁍ John Calvin (1509-1564)[114]

day 36

speak

SPEAK up for those who cannot speak for themselves....
Psalm 31:8 NCV

*W*alking through pouring rain from the dining hall to the gym, I followed the long line of wheelchairs rolling down the muddy path. *How miserable this must be for them,* I thought.

And yet, each drenched camper was smiling and I never heard one complaint.

They were just so thrilled for the opportunity to be in a beautiful camp for a whole week with family, friends, helpers, recreation, great food, fun activities, and spiritual enrichment. In fact, most of these adults called this the best week of their whole year—"Joni and Friends Family Camp New England."

Mike and I were honored to be serving all week as pastor-in-residence and had brought our own adult son to participate as a camper. Though it was a rainy week, we will never forget the lessons we learned from our fellow campers and their families.

We were there to teach and encourage them. In reality, we became the receivers.

And it never would have happened if a teenage girl hadn't broken her neck after a dive into a swimming hole more than forty-five years ago.

Joni Eareckson Tada, the founder and CEO of Joni and Friends, is an international advocate for people with disabilities and one of my personal heroes. A diving accident in 1967 left her a quadriplegic in a wheelchair. After two years of rehabilitation and a lot of soul searching, she emerged with new skills and a fresh determination to help others in similar situations.

She decided to "speak up for the rights of all who need an advocate."

Since its inception, Joni and Friends has been dedicated to extending the love and message of Christ to people who are affected by disability whether it is the disabled person, a family member, or friend. Their objective is to meet the physical, emotional, and spiritual needs of this group of people in practical ways through recruiting, training, and motivating new generations of people with disabilities to become leaders in their churches and communities.

Family camps are just one of many ministries that help toward this end. Throughout the years, Joni has served on the National Council on Disability and the Disability Advisory Committee to the U.S. State Department. She has helped guide evangelism strategies among people with disabilities worldwide and received numerous awards and honors, including the Victory Award from the National Rehabilitation Hospital and the Golden Word Award from the International Bible Society. Joni has been awarded several honorary degrees, including Doctor of Divinity from Westminster Theological Seminary; Doctor of Humanitarian Services from California Baptist University; and Doctor of Humane Letters by Indiana University. In 2012, the Colson Center on Christian Worldview awarded Joni its prestigious "William Wilberforce Award."

It took courage for Joni and her husband, Ken, to move beyond their own challenges toward a redemptive ministry for others going through similar struggles. But because they chose to *speak,* thousands of people worldwide will never be the same again.

In addition to family camps, another essential work is Wheels for the World, which provides wheelchairs (refurbished by prison inmates) for people living in developing countries all over the world. Joni explains, "I may be a quadriplegic, but I simply can't sit still when I know there are people out there are who suffering far more than I ever will. God has blessed me with amazing health and strength, and I need to 'pass on the blessings' to other people with disabilities who are crawling in the dirt, languishing in bed, or stuck in dreary institutions.

"Why should I enjoy the luxury of two wheelchairs when there are disabled people like me who have none? How can I enjoy the glorious benefits of the Gospel of Christ, and not also care about people who've never even heard His Gospel? Wheels for the World helps give people with disabilities hope in Christ, and a much-coveted wheelchair. We are driven by God's heart of compassion for the helpless, for 'He raises the poor from the dust and lifts the needy from the ash heap' (Psalm 113:7). 'Arise, Lord! Lift up your hand, O God. Do not forget the helpless'" (Psalm 10:12).[115]

In the Bible, we find an account of King David also speaking up once he discovered his dear friend Jonathan's son, Mephibosheth. In 2 Samuel chapter 9, David is seeking anyone from the family of Saul and Jonathan to whom he may show kindness. He learns through a servant that when Jonathan died, he left a five-year-old son who was lame in both legs. At once David sends for the now-grown Mephibosheth who is surprised at the king's warm welcome.

After a lifetime of being overlooked, he bows to his king and says, "What is your servant, that you should notice a dead dog like me?" (2 Samuel 9:8).

But David is determined to bestow dignity on him and honor both Saul and Jonathan's memory by making the rest of Mephibosheth's life more comfortable. "'Don't be afraid,' David said to him, 'for I will surely show you kindness for the sake of your father Jonathan. I will restore to you all the land that belonged to your grandfather Saul, and you will always eat at my table'" (2 Samuel 9:7). David set him and his family up for life with servants and land.

The story ends by once again pointing out that Mephibosheth "lived in Jerusalem, because he always ate at the king's table; he was lame in both feet" (2 Samuel 9:13).

When God's people decide to make an active response to His Word, they can literally change the world. Consider others who chose to *speak* after their lives were upended in one way or another. Gary Haugen was a lawyer working for the U.S. Department of Justice when he was sent to Rwanda to direct a team of criminal prosecutors, forensic experts, and law enforcement investigating the widespread genocide. These experiences were what compelled him to begin the International Justice Mission, a human rights agency that brings rescue to victims of slavery, sexual exploitation, and other forms of violent oppression.

After serving time in a federal prison for Watergate activities, newly committed Christian Charles Colson founded Prison Fellowship. This was to honor a promise he made to remember prisoners and their families. That promise grew into the world's largest family of prison ministries. My dear friends Gene and Carol Kent also started a ministry to prisoners' families, Speak Up for Hope, after their only son was sentenced to life in prison without parole. Their ministry, based on our scripture today, exists to provide hope to inmates and their families through encouragement and resources.

Eunice Kennedy Shriver had a sister, Rosemary, who was born with intellectual disabilities and therefore shut out of participation in any kind of organized sports. In her efforts to *speak,* Eunice and her family started the Special Olympics, which allows people with intellectual disabilities to discover new strengths and abilities, skills, and success through the power of sports. Special Olympics athletes find joy, confidence, and fulfillment—on the playing field and in life. Our own family involvement can testify that these athletes indeed inspire people in their communities to open their hearts to a wider world of human talents and potential.

All around us are people who are living on the fringe of society and do not have a voice. Too often they are overlooked. But God's people should be different. We should lead the way in giving a voice to the voiceless.

It's time to *speak.*

live these words

Do you know someone who needs an advocate? Begin by honoring one person as an individual created in the image of God -- someone whom others tend to ignore or demean. Spend time with them, talking and getting to know what their life is really like. Then pray for guidance on how you might *speak* on behalf of those with a particular challenge.

Try this twelfth-century prayer from Anselm: *We bring before You, O Lord, the troubles and perils of peoples and nations, the frustration of prisoners and captives, the anguish of the bereaved, the needs of refugees, the helplessness of the weak, the despondency of the weary, the failing powers of the aged and the hopelessness of the starving. O Lord, draw near to each, for the sake of Jesus Christ our Lord. Amen.*

I mentioned five different people whose work came about as a result of their personal challenges and involvement. Though not an exhaustive list by any means, it's a place to start.

JoniandFriends.org

IJM.org (International Justice Mission)

PrisonFellowship.org

SpeakUpforHope.org

SpecialOlympics.org

pray these words

Let us now go forth into the world in peace.
Being of good courage.
Holding fast to that which is good.
Rendering to no one evil for evil.
Strengthening the faint-hearted.
Supporting the weak.
Helping the afflicted.
Honoring all persons.
Loving and serving the Lord.
And rejoicing in the power of the Holy Spirit.
Amen.

⁎ Common Commission of First Church of Christ
Congregational, Wethersfield, Connecticut[116]

day 37

encourage

...*ENCOURAGE* one another and build each other up, just as in fact you are doing. 1 Thessalonians 5:11

*H*ow much farther to the top?" I panted to my hiking companions. My Furman friends and I loved to spend weekends climbing in the Great Smokey Mountains, but I inevitably seemed to drift into that unenviable position of bringing up the rear.

"Not too far, Secrest. You can make it. Keep going," one of them yelled down.

I turned and leaned my backpack against the incline, gazing at the autumn palette of color vividly displayed on the valley below. How could the view higher up be any better than this?

"Look y'all! Turn around. From here it looks like the top to me! Couldn't we just pretend we're already at the summit?" I pleaded.

Desperate for a rest, I was quite willing to accept this partial view as a reward for our day's climb.

If I had, I would have missed so much.

A grander panorama of beauty awaited me at the peak. A celebration of friends reaching the top together. A feeling of accomplishment for having completed the journey.

To this day, old college friends still tease me, "Remember, Secrest? 'Looks like the top to *me*!'" they laugh.

But actually it's a sobering thought to think that I almost gave up before reaching the summit.

What they did was to *encourage* me—to keep going. They fleshed out that word that means "to inspire courage in another person." The right words of affirmation and support spoken at the right time can offer just the courage another needs to take important and meaningful steps in life.

And I'm not just talking about climbing mountains.

My first and favorite devotional as a teenager was called *Streams in the Desert*. In it, Mrs. Charles Cowman illustrates what it means to be an encourager with this poem, "Call Back."

If you have gone a little way ahead of me,
call back—
'Twill cheer my heart and help my feet
along the stony track;

And if, perchance, Faith's light is dim,
because the oil is low,
Your call will guide my lagging course
as wearily I go.
Call back, and tell me that He went
with you into the storm;
Call back, and say He kept you
when the forest's roots were torn;
That, when the heavens thunder
and the earthquake shook the hill,
He bore you up and held you
where the very air was still.
Oh, friend, call back, and tell me
for I cannot see your face,
They say it glows with triumph,
and your feet bound in the race;
But there are mists between us
and my spirit eyes are dim,
And I cannot see the glory,
though I long for word of Him.
But if you'll say He heard you
when your prayer was but a cry,
And if you'll say He saw you
through the night's sin-darkened sky
If you have gone a little way ahead,
oh, friend, call back—
'Twill cheer my heart and help my feet
along the stony track.[117]

I determined early in life that I would be one who calls back—living the words *encourage each other and build each other up.*

Because I knew how much I thrived on encouragement.

In the four love languages, my own language of love is "words of affirmation," and so I readily relate to the biblical mandate, "You must encourage one another each day. And you must keep on while there is still time…" (Hebrews 3:13 CEV). The Greek verb here is *parakaleo*, which means "to encourage or comfort, to come alongside, to beseech." It appears in the imperative and is a continually commanded action—keep on encouraging.

Words are powerful tools. They can build up. They can crush. Paul reminds us that we should use words to encourage, "…encourage one another with these words" (1 Thessalonians 4:18).

What words?

Well, to begin with, words that remind us we are truly loved. Perhaps the best words of encouragement any of us will ever hear are, "God loves you."

Henri Nouwen once said, "The best gift my friendship can give to you is the gift of your belovedness." Each of us is God's beloved, but often our encouragement is needed to help others claim that identity. That is how we learn to recognize the voice of love that speaks into our hearts and to tune out all other voices, which try to define us by their approval or disapproval.

"When we speak to each other, reminding one another of our uniqueness, we come to realize that we do offer something no one else offers. This is why reminding and affirming one another of being the beloved is so vitally important. Community is the place where this should happen. In our competitive workplaces, schools, and world, we won't hear much talk about love. These are the places where the language of being the beloved competes with the language of earned acceptance. Our various communities—healthy families; safe friendships; churches—are where we look forward to being accepted, embraced, touched, and recognized for who we are."[118]

Being in relationship is essential because there is no way we can encourage someone else unless we are aware of their lives—struggles, challenges, and feelings. We need to be involved and to listen actively, and yes, even to sometimes ask the hard questions. Generally, encouraging words are ones that communicate the idea *I know who you are; I care about you,* and *I'm here to help you.*

C. S. Lewis once said, "Friendship is born at that moment when one person says to another, 'What! You too? I thought I was the only one.'" Sharing words of encouragement shows others they are not alone.

When was the last time you had that "You too?" moment?

I'm so thankful my friends cheered me to the top of the mountain that day so long ago. But I'm even more grateful for other voices through the years that have believed in me, even when I didn't believe in myself. Those who took action and reached down to lift me up when I fell.

The softest voice that resonated the loudest was Jesus extending His grace to me—a gift I didn't deserve and could never earn. When I finally opened that gift—truly received His grace—my whole life changed. Recognizing myself as the beloved, helped me to stop judging, stop performing, stop striving. After embracing the grace extended from above (vertical), I began to live out grace to all around me (horizontal).

Sadly, I don't always get it right.

Sometimes my words and actions *dis*courage, instead of encourage, but God's grace reminds me that there is always a second chance to try again.

There is always an opportunity to turn around, face the mountain, and keep climbing.

I choose to live out encouraging words, not because my words are so important, but because they are rooted in God's Word.

Filtered through me, they somehow give life.

live these words

There are endless ways to encourage other people. Here are a few from *Practicing Affirmation:*

- ❧ Commend someone for the way (sensitivity, kindness, compassion, etc.) with which he treated a third party. You noticed, and so does God.

- ❧ Quote someone positively in his presence. "I agree with Jacob here, who said...."

- ❧ Get up from your chair, go to another room, seek out a person, and simply say something like, "I just came to say, 'Good morning.'"

- ❧ At a committee or board meeting, before moving on to the next agenda item, stop to commend those who worked on the previous item.

- ❧ Just as God decisively chose Paul (Acts 9), tell your spouse, "I chose you, and I still do."

- Loan something of value—books, camping gear, a car, a cabin—as a signal of your willingness to take a risk, having noticed something in the other person that elevates your confidence in her trustworthiness.

- When asked to do a chore, consider saying something like, "Nothing would give me more pleasure right now than doing this for you." Serving someone can be affirming of them.

- Nominate someone for an office or post—based upon her integrity, dependability, or trustworthiness.

- Ask someone's advice.

- Commend the wisdom and helpfulness of a suggestion someone made, especially when they have offered to be a part of a solution to a problem.

- Write a personal letter or note card that an employee can take home or put in a personnel file. Keep a supply of such blank note cards in your desk for just such a purpose.[119]

pray these words

Thank you, Lord, for the ways You fashion my life around relationships. Were it not for my family and friends, I would find myself so alone in this world. As I continue to reflect on the quality of my relationships, help me identify ways I can continually be a positive contributor to the health and well-being of others. May the love, mercy, grace and compassion of Jesus be my daily source of strength and hope. I long to be Your ambassador of peace and reconciliation in my family, among my friendships, and in the various communities where You lead me to love and serve others. In Your name, Father, Son and Holy Spirit, and for Your kingdom's sake. Amen.

                                                ∽ Stephen A. Macchia[120]

day 38

STAY here and keep watch with Me. Matthew 26:38

*D*addy was dying. Slipping away. Struggling. Sleeping more than staying awake. Trying so hard to hold on to this life and his loved ones, while also longing for the peace and rest promised in heaven.

I sang hymns to him, held him, read Scripture, read his own poetry, and played recordings of his own piano music.

But mostly I just sat.

I wanted to run screaming into the night, *God, why are You letting Daddy suffer? Please deliver him from pain. I already miss him so much.*

But I didn't run. I stayed.

Vigil. It's a hard word.

The dictionary says it means "a period of keeping awake during the time usually spent asleep, especially to keep watch or pray." I think of vigil as the ministry of presence—just being with someone while they are going through a hard time.

Sometimes all we can offer is our presence.

And sometimes that is enough.

Years ago I was a member of a Sunday school class taught by Joe Bayly, a delightful man who, after burying three sons, penned *The View from a Hearse*. I've never forgotten his words about the importance of vigil in the life of someone in pain: "I was sitting, torn by grief. Someone came and talked to me of God's dealings, of why it happened, of hope beyond the grave. He talked constantly. He said things I knew were true. I was unmoved, except to wish he'd go away. He finally did.

"Another came and sat beside me. He didn't talk. He didn't ask me leading questions. He just sat beside me for an hour or more, listened when I said something, answered briefly, prayed simply, left. I was moved. I was comforted. I hated to see him go."[121]

Perhaps this is what Jesus needed when he beckoned his friends, "Stay."

The disciples had joined Him in the Garden of Gethsemane after the Last Supper. After Judas had run away to do his betraying. But they were exhausted and one by one, they fell asleep.

Jesus knows what's coming and He struggles with facing it alone.

He calls out to God, "My Father, if it is possible, may this cup be taken from me (Matthew 26:39). He'd rather not walk through the suffering He knows is ahead of Him. Then He reaches deep to trust in the Father who loves Him,

"Yet not as I will, but as you will" (Matthew 26:39).

Still, He longs for companionship in the crisis, comfort in the calm before the storm. Thus His entreaty, "Stay." *Don't fall asleep on me now, boys, not when I most need to know you have my back. Don't leave me. It will be enough to just know you are waiting here with me, keeping vigil for what is coming next.*

Jesus appears quite alone in the garden and the ensuing trial and crucifixion. "My God, my God, why have you forsaken me?" (Matthew 27:46). As He took the sins of the world upon Himself on the cross, the physical pain was immense, but the spiritual ache was even greater.

Love demanded a price.

I've often wondered what I would have done that weekend had I been one of Christ's closest friends. Would I have fallen asleep or kept vigil? Would I have offered to help carry His cross? Would I have made myself scarce or stood beside Him all the way?

Though I could not be with Jesus at Calvary, I can do what He asked. I can offer the ministry of my own presence to others who feel alone in their suffering, dying, confusion, or persecution.

I can do what Joe Bayly's friend did and just show up.

Sit.

Pray.

Keep watch.

God does this with us throughout our lives. He promises His presence every moment of every day. We may feel alone. It may look like we are alone.

But we are never alone. "Never will I leave you; never will I forsake you" (Hebrews 13:5).

live these words

Perhaps there will be a time you can give the gift of vigil with someone who is in pain or dying. But it is also important to learn how to practice God's constant presence in your own life. In *The Book of the Hours* (1513) we are encouraged to repeat this litany:

> *Through every moment of this day: You are with me Lord. Through every day of all this week: You are with me Lord. Through every week of all this year: You are with me Lord. Through every year of all this life: You are with me Lord. So that when time is past, By grace I may at last be with You, Lord. Amen.*[122]

Here are some practical steps you can take to experience more deeply the presence of God:

1. If you can't sense God's presence, there may be something in your life that is blocking the communication. Search your soul, confess your sins, and ask Him to give you an ear to hear His voice again.

2. Play praise music or Scripture put to music and soak in God's Truth, singing your own hymns of praise. Read your Bible aloud and listen to all the promises as though God were speaking them just to you.

3. Pray constantly. Practice "breathe prayers" where you send up simple heartfelt petitions to Him, such as, *"Lord, I need You,"* or *"Send Your grace and*

mercy." Also, take time in complete silence to just be in the presence of God. Listen to that still small voice. As you breathe deeply, exhale worries, and inhale His peace.

4. Take a walk and experience God's creation and say or sing your praises "in the name of Jesus" to honor and adore Him. If you are walking around your neighborhood, pray a blessing on each house you pass.

pray these words

Abide with me; fast falls the eventide; The darkness deepens; Lord with me abide. When other helpers fail and comforts flee, Help of the helpless, O abide with me.

Swift to its close ebbs out life's little day; Earth's joys grow dim; its glories pass away; Change and decay in all around I see; O Thou who changest not, abide with me.

Come not in terrors, as the King of kings, But kind and good, with healing in Thy wings, Tears for all woes, a heart for every plea—Come, Friend of sinners, and thus bide with me.

I need Thy presence every passing hour. What but Thy grace can foil the tempter's power? Who, like Thyself, my guide and stay can be? Through cloud and sunshine, Lord, abide with me.

Hold Thou Thy cross before my closing eyes; Shine through the gloom and point me to the skies. Heaven's morning breaks, and earth's vain shadows flee; In life, in death, O Lord, abide with me. Amen.

ഇ Henry F. Lyte (1847)[123]

day 39

love

...LOVE each other deeply, because love covers over a multitude of sins. 1 Peter 4:8

I remember praying that we would make it to our tenth wedding anniversary.

Marriage had been challenging from the get-go. Of course, there were perfectly good reasons why this was so, but that didn't lessen my subtle feelings of failure to discover the key to this mystery. We loved each other, loved our four children, and had made a covenant to one another and God, in front of witnesses, "till death do us part."

So every day became a decision to *do* what God said—*love each other deeply.*

We already had the whole *multitude of sins* thing covered because there was no doubt that each of us had married a sinner. But it was the pro-active verb to *love* that was the deciding factor.

We had to choose to act on our commitment, whether we felt like it or not.

This year we celebrate our thirtieth anniversary.

I have never loved Mike more deeply than I do now. Deep, as in soul-level. We continue to grow into the very people that we vowed so long ago to encourage each other to become. Life has certainly sanded off a lot of rough edges in the process.

I've thought a lot about married love this past year, especially since I've been involved in five family weddings. My heart fills with joy as I see the bride and groom eager to begin their lives together. I want all good things for them, and my prayers are that they won't have to go through any struggles or challenges along the way to their own thirtieth anniversaries.

But I realize that may be unrealistic in today's culture where many people look at marriage as more of a contract *(I will love you as long as you fulfill the need I have right now, but when you can't, I'm out of here.)* than a covenant *(My love for you is a binding relationship of love and commitment which takes precedence over my changing needs and desires.)*.

Because sometimes it takes a lifetime to make it to that deep kind of loving. It's not the same as the love we felt on our wedding day. It is a love that covers the inevitable times when our spouse disappoints us or rejects us.

What do we do on those days? When feelings of affection and delight cannot be sustained?

Authors Tim and Kathy Keller (married thirty-nine years) of Manhattan's Redeemer Church answer this way.

> When that happens you must remember that the essence of a marriage is that it is a covenant, a commitment, a promise of future love. So what do you do? You *do* the acts of love, despite your lack of feeling. You may not feel tender, sympathetic, and eager to please, but in your actions you must *be* tender, understanding, forgiving, and helpful. And, if you do that, as time goes on you will not only get through the dry spells, but you will become more constant in your feelings. This is what can happen if you decide to love.[124]

My greatest advice for anyone considering marriage is to remember that the healthiest unions are when two whole people come together—men and women who retain their unique individuality on so many levels, but who make a deliberate choice to join their lives and resources in order to be even more for the kingdom. Don't look for your better half. Do everything you can to grow into wholeness, so you bring that person together with another who is also whole.

Oswald Chambers and his wife, Biddy, are a good example of deep loving. We remember him as the author of a classic devotional *My Utmost for His Highest*. But he never actually wrote that book. What Oswald did was give many, many spiritual talks to young people and soldiers, encouraging them in their faith. And his wife, Biddy, carefully wrote down each word as he spoke. This act of selflessness made it possible for his books to be compiled and therefore shared with many generations to follow.

Biddy recorded her husband's words because she wanted to partner with him in ministry. Chambers' biographer describes their unique marriage, "They encouraged each other by walking individually with God and finding His grace sufficient to meet their needs. Together, their lives intertwined into a cord of shared ministry that was stronger than either could have woven alone."[125]

A few years ago Mike and I renewed our wedding vows on our friends' back patio. I wore my wedding gown, and our attendants were our four young adult children. As we stood there, it seemed appropriate that our kids were now witnessing the very vows that they had each spent a quarter of a century watching us seek to fulfill.

I held a copy of our original wedding bulletin and repeated, "...and I do promise and covenant before God and these witnesses to be your faithful and loving wife, in joy and in sorrow, in plenty and in want, in health and in sickness, to love, cherish, and support you as head of our marriage, directing our family to Christ who is head of the church. I honor you as a unique and gifted man of God and promise to encourage you to become all God has created you to be. This I freely and gladly choose to do in obedience to Christ who is Lord in everything, till death do us part, according to God's holy law. This is my solemn vow."

I thought back to my own parents who had made similar vows and, though they were absolute opposites, managed with grace to keep those vows for sixty-two years until death parted them. How grateful I am for that legacy, one that I hope to pass along to our own children.

God makes a covenant with us and we, in turn, make covenants with one another. Glancing at my wedding bulletin, I notice the scripture Mike and I claimed on that special day—a reminded of God's lasting covenant. "They will be my people, and I will be their God. I will give them singleness of heart and action, so that they will always fear me and that all will then go well for them and for their children after them. I will make an everlasting covenant with them: I will never stop doing good to them,.... I will rejoice in doing them good and will assuredly plant them in this land with all my heart and soul" (Jeremiah 32:38-41).

And so I continue to *love* deeply.

live these words

Our word today—*love*—encompasses so much more than just marital love. I know that. I also know that for some readers, marital love did not endure for a variety of reasons. I still decided to write on deep love that *covers a multitude of sins* within the framework of marriage for the many of us who still grapple with that important reality. Do keep in mind, however, that when it comes to loving, these are certainly transferable principles that are helpful in many different relationships.

The disciple whom Jesus *loved* (close friendship) wrote "No one has ever seen God; but if we love one another, God lives in us and his love is made complete in us" (1 John 4:12). So think about who you need to *love* and what that deep love should look like. Write down descriptive words that come to mind and then begin to do them. That's how we will know that God is living in us.

pray these words

O Lord Jesus Christ our God, our Sweet Savior,
Who taught us to pray always for each other,
so that by thus fulfilling the holy law we will

be made worthy of Thy mercy: look down with compassion on our married life and keep from all perilous falls, from enemies both visible and invisible, my husband/wife whom Thou hast granted me, that we may pass our time together until the end with oneness of mind. Grant him/her health, strength, and fullness of wisdom enlightened from above, so that he/she may be able to fulfill his/her duties all the days of this life according to Thy will and commandments.

Protect and keep him/her from temptations, and may he/she be able to bear and conquer those temptations that come upon him/her. Strengthen him/her in right faith, strong hope, and perfect love, so that together we may do good deeds and that we may order all our life according to Thy divine commandments.

O Merciful Lord, hear us who humbly pray to Thee, and send Thy divine blessing in truth on our married life and on all our good deeds, for it is Thine to hear and have mercy on us, O our God, and to Thee we ascribe glory: to the Father and to the Son and to the Holy Spirit, both now and ever, and unto ages of ages. Amen.

ò Orthodox Prayer for Marriage[126]

day 40

consecrate

CONSECRATE yourselves, for tomorrow the Lord
will do wonders among you. Joshua 3:5 ESV

Sometimes it takes a few attempts before we see the wonders.

Joshua had already tried to get into the Promised Land. As young men, he and Caleb had spied out the situation and determined that with the help of the almighty God, the Israelites could prevail. Nonetheless, their hope-filled predictions were drowned out by pessimistic comrades, now forever remembered as the "ten faithless spies." Numbers 13 and 14 reveal how harshly God dealt with the Israelites' lack of courage and faith.

As a result, God's chosen ones wandered in the desert for forty more years.

Forty long years.

The price of fear. The price of listening to and heeding the wrong voices. The price of underestimating the power of the same God who had just miraculously parted the Red Sea.

The first generation that left captivity in Egypt chose to play it safe. Despite all the miracles they had seen, the deliverance they had experienced, and the manna that had been provided, they continued to complain, choosing fear rather than faith when the opportunity arose.

And a whole lot of time was wasted.

Do you and I have forty more years to wander around? Forty more years to keep doing the same old thing, expecting different results?

Or are we at a point where we know that the God who calls is also the God who will provide?

Moses died before he ever saw his dreams come to fruition. But God chose to give Joshua another opportunity to take a new generation into Canaan, and this time nothing could stand in his way.

When God called Joshua, He reminded him three times to *be strong and courageous* (See Joshua 1:6-9). Then, acting on that strength and courage for leading these people into their destiny, Joshua in turn charged them to *consecrate yourselves, for tomorrow the Lord will do wonders among you.*

To *consecrate* means "to set apart for a special or sacred purpose." Bread and wine are consecrated for communion. Churches are consecrated for worship.

You and I are consecrated—set apart—for what purpose? That the Lord might do wonders among us.

But only as we step out in faith, eyes on the prize.

When the time comes to cross the Jordan, God plans to make a way. If the people are willing to step into the river. God's promise is that as soon as the priests' feet rest in the Jordan, *then* the waters will part.

Who is brave enough to take that first step? During the harvest floods, the rolling river is a mile wide. These folks have spent their whole lifetime in the desert and are already understandably overwhelmed with the rushing waters.

What's more, this command is a one-two punch. One is being willing to be set apart—*consecrated*—for God's use. But two is being willing to step out to claim that promise when everything in you screams that what you are attempting is virtually impossible.

For some of us, that's when the bargaining begins: "You go first, God. Just reveal to me that person/job/ministry and then I'll be happy to comply."

But God replies, "No, you go first. Move forward in the direction I'm calling you. Take a leap of faith and then I'll reveal to you the specific person/job/ministry."

"For heaven's sake, get your feet wet!"

How sad if we decide to play it safe. Do we really want to be one who spends our entire life on the eastern banks of the Jordan River? So very close to the dream, the promise, the miracle, but unwilling to take the first step.

We encounter many rivers as we journey through life. When God beckons from the farthest bank, do we trust Him? Or do we waste time wandering in our own desert places?

Today you may be called to cross over to something completely different, to leave your old life behind and strike out in a new direction with His blessing, to do things for

Him you've never done before. But He guarantees you His presence, power, and provision. Isn't that enough?

Fortunately, those priests were desperate enough to go for it. And when the twelve placed their feet in the middle of the overflowing river, more than forty thousand Israelites crossed on dry land to a whole new life.

A memorial was established on the banks of Gilgal—twelve stones from the riverbed placed by members of each of the twelve tribes. This was done so that everyone would always remember two wonders: that Israel crossed on dry ground (what seemed impossible) and that the Lord's hand is mighty (what He promises, He fulfills) (Joshua 4:20-24).

What is your dream? Where do you need a miracle? What promise will you claim? What new ground will you take?

Consecrate yourself. Trust God. Step into the river.

And prepare for wonders.

live these words

On this fortieth day of *living the words*, you know the routine. It's not enough to just read about what God says in His Word, we need to *respond in an active way*. We need to reflect on others' stories and allow truth to be woven into our own stories.

What did you take away from Joshua today? On which side of the Jordan River will you choose to live? Do two things: *Consecrate* your life through prayer (just as John Wesley did and many wonders followed), then target one risky step you could take toward fulfilling your God-given destiny.

And after the wonders come, be sure and place some stones of remembrance so you can remind others of your great God and what He did.

pray these words

> *Lord God, I am no longer my own, but Yours. Put me to what You will, rank me with whom You will; put me to doing, put me to suffering; let me be employed for You, or laid aside for You, exalted for You, or brought low for You, let me be full, let me be empty, let me have all things, let me have nothing: I freely and wholeheartedly yield all things to Your pleasure and disposal. And now, glorious and blessed God, Father, Son and Holy Spirit, You are mine and I am Yours. So be it. And the covenant now made on earth, let it be ratified in heaven. Amen.*

> ⁞ John Wesley (1703-1791)[127]

Every word You give me is a miracle word—how could I help but obey? Break open Your words, let the light shine out, let ordinary people see their meaning.
Psalm 119:129-130 THE MESSAGE

about the author

Lucinda Secrest McDowell is a storyteller whose greatest joy is making God's faithfulness visible through practical illustrations of biblical truth in ordinary life. In addition to *Live These Words*, she has authored ten other books, including *Amazed by Grace, 30 Ways to Embrace Life, God's Purpose for You, Role of a Lifetime,* and *Spa for the Soul.*

She is also a contributing author to 25 books and has published in more than 50 different magazines, earning Mt. Hermon's "Writer of the Year" award.

Cindy holds degrees from Gordon-Conwell Theological Seminary and Furman University and also studied at the Wheaton Graduate School of Communication. Through her ministry "Encouraging Words," she brings enthusiastic wit and wisdom as an international conference speaker and seminar teacher. Active in several different professional communities, she is also a co-director of the annual "New England Christian Writers Retreat." In addition to her husband and children, Cindy enjoys tea parties, letters on fine stationery, cozy quilts, good books, country music, bright colors, ancient prayers, and laughing friends. A southerner from birth, she now writes from "Sunnyside" cottage in a small New England town. Visit her at EncouragingWords.net

My mission is to glorify God and live in His grace and freedom, and through the power of the Holy Spirit, to use my gifts to communicate God's faithfulness, extend His grace, and encourage others to trust Him fully.   L.S.M.

Connect with Cindy on

  Lucinda Secrest McDowell

  @LucindaSMcDowel

<u>Contact</u>: Lucinda Secrest McDowell

Encouraging Words
P.O. Box 290707
Wethersfield, CT 06129 USA
Phone: 860.529.7175
Email: cindy@encouragingwords.net
Website/Blog: www.EncouragingWords.net

For further questions, contact
Bold Vision Books
PO Box 2011
Friendswood, Texas 77549

www.boldvisionbooks.com

Endnotes

1. Anonymous, *The Cloud of Unknowing*, 1375. http://www. ccel.org/ (Christian Classics Ethereal Library)
2. *Book of Common Prayer*, The Episcopal Church. New York, 1979. http://www.bcponline.org/
3. A.A. Milne, *Winnie the Pooh*. www.goodreads.com/work/ quotes/1225592-winnie-the-pooh.
4. Will L. Thompson "Softly and Tenderly" (public domain) in Hymns for the Family of God, Nashville, TN: Paragon Associates, 1976. p. 432.
5. Ruth Myers, *A Treasury of Praise*, Colorado Springs CO: Multnomah Books, 2007. p. 61
6. Ruth Myers, ibid. p. 169.
7. Eric Metaxas, *Everything You Always Wanted to Know About God*, Colorado Springs CO: WaterBrook Press, 2005. p. 179.
8. Eric Metaxas, ibid. p. 175.
9. My family always named our houses, even though we never had mansions or estates. There was often a story behind the name and it was occasionally tied to a Scriptural promise from God. When Mike and I married, we decided to carry on this tradition.
10. Scotty Smith, The Gospel Coalition. http:// thegospelcoalition.org/blogs/scottysmith/2013/08/11/a-prayer-4-trusting-god-4-fresh-peach-and-straight-paths/
11. Rebecca M. Pippert, *Hope Has Its Reasons*, Downers Grove IL: InterVarsity Press, 2001.
12. Frederich Buechner, "An Easter Prayer" in *From Death to Life*, Christian Communications for the Parish. out of print.
13. Max Lucado, *Fearless*, Nashville TN: Thomas Nelson, 2009.
14. Jonathan Aitken, *Prayers for People Under Pressure*, Wheaton IL: Crossway Books, 2008. p. 154.
15. Amy Carmichael, "Nothing in the House," in *Toward Jerusalem*, copyright 1936 by the Dohnavur Fellowship. Used by permission of CLC Publications. May not be further reproduced. All rights reserved.

16. Celtic Prayer in *Power Lines:* Celtic Prayers about Work. Edited by Davis Adam. Harrisburg, PA: Moorehouse, 1992

17. Brother Lawrence, *The Practice of the Presence of God,* Spiritual Matters Series. New York NY: Paulist Press, 1978.

18. Francis de Sales quoted in *Near To The Heart of God,* compiled by Bernard Bagley, Wheaton IL: Harold Shaw Publishers, 1998. April 27 entry.

19. John R. W. Stott, http://thegospelcoalition.org/blogs/trevinwax/2010/03/21/john-stotts-morning-trinitarian-prayer/

20. David Adam, *The Rhythm of Life*, Harrisburg PA: Morehouse Publishing, 2007. p. 104.

21. Elisabeth Elliot, *God's Guidance*, Grand Rapids MI: Revell, 2006.

22. Anonymous Prayer, www.scrapbook.com/poems/doc/6108.html

23. Thomas Merton, *Thoughts in Solitude*, New York NY: Farrar, Straus & Giroux, 1999.

24. Suzanne Phillips, "Teens Sleeping with Cell Phones," www.pbs.org/thisemotionallife/blogs/

25. Ruth Haley Barton, *Sacred Rhythms*, Downers Grove IL: InterVarsity Press, 2006. p. 23.

26. Jennifer Kennedy Dean, *Live A Praying Life*, Birmingham AL: New Hope Publishers, 2010. p. 97.

27. Stephen W. Smith, *Embracing Soul Care*, Grand Rapids MI: Kregel Publishers, 2006. p. 223.

28. Mark Batterson, *The Circle Maker*, Grand Rapids MI: Zondervan, 2011. p. 195.

29. Richard Foster, *Prayer: Finding the Heart's True Home*, San Francisco CA: HarperCollins, 1992. p. 24-25.

30. Ann Voskamp, http://www.aholyexperience.com/

31. George Herbert prayer in *The Communion of Saints: Prayers of the Famous,* edited by Horton Davies. Grand Rapids MI: Eerdmans, 1990.

32. Ann Voskamp, *One Thousand Gifts Devotional*, Grand Rapids MI: Zondervan, 2012. p. 9.

33. Augustine Confession Prayer quoted in *Near To The Heart of God,* compiled by Bernard Bagley, Wheaton, IL: Harold Shaw Publishers, 1998. October 3 entry.

34. Thorton Wilder, *Our Town*. http://www.stageagent.com/Shows/Monologues/view/986.

35. http://www.sixwordmemoirs.com/

36. Lucinda Secrest McDowell, *Role of a Lifetime,* Nashville TN: B & H Publishing, 2008. p. 50.

37. Mitch Albom, *Tuesdays with Morrie,.* www.goodreads.com/work/quotes/1995335-tuesdays-with-morrie

38. Randy Pausch, *The Last Lecture,.* www.goodreads.com/author/quotes/287960.Randy_Pausch

39. John Baillie, *A Diary of Private Prayer*, London: Oxford Univeristy Press, 1936. p. 41.

40. Francis de Sales, *Introduction to the Devout Life*, translated by John K. Ryan, Garden City NY: Doubleday, 1972.

41. Dietrich Bonhoeffer prayer, *The Book of a Thousand Prayers*, compiled by Angela Ashwin. Grand Rapids MI: Zondervan, 1996. p. 38.

42. "The Real St. Patrick," by Franciscan Media Editors. http://www.americancatholic.org/

43. Flavius Josephus, *The Jewish War* Vol. III, Harvard University Press, 1997. p. 27.

44. St. Patrick's Breastplate, www.ourcatholicprayers.com/st-patricks-breastplate.html

45. Tommy Nelson, "Anxiety Attack," *Leadership Journal*, Winter 2013. pp. 87-91.

46. World Health Organization article. www.who.int/topics/depression/en/

47. Anonymous prayer handed to me a few years ago. I have not been able to discover the author.

48. William Tyndale, "Exposition on the Sermon on the Mount," (16th century) public domain.

49. Robert Benson, *A Good Life*, Brewster MA: Paraclete Press, 2004. p. 66.

50. Teresa of Avila prayer, *Hear Our Prayer*, Peabody MA: Hendrickson Publishers, 2004. p. 70.

51. Ken Gire, *Moments with the Savior*, Grand Rapids MI: Zondervan, 1998. pp. 272-273.

52. Mark Batterson, *The Circle Maker*, ibid. p. 56.

53. Prayer of St. Clement, www.catholic.org/prayers/prayer. php?p=223

54. Michael Inbar, "Groundhog Day for Real," Today online, 8/6/2010.

55. Kay Arthur, *As Silver Refined*, Colorado Springs CO: WaterBrook Press, 2011.

56. Tessa Afshar, *Peal in the Sand*, Chicago IL: Moody Publishers, 2010. p. 284.

57. Charles Swindoll, *Growing Strong in the Seasons of Life*, Portland OR: Multnomah Press, 1983. p. 374.

58. Ruth Myers, ibid. p. 78.

59. Hildegarde of Bingen, www.christianitytoday.com/ch/ content/quote.html

60. Robert Lowery, "How Can I Keep From Singing," public domain. www.cyberhymnal.org/htm/h/c/hcaikeep.htm

61. "Prayer for Church Musicians and Artists," *Book of Common Prayer*, ibid. http:// www.bcponline.org/misc/ prayers.htm#17

62. Stephen Curtis Chapman and Scotty Smith, *Restoring Broken Things*, Nashville TN: Integrity Publishers, 2005. p. 134.

63. June Hunt, *Forgiveness, the Freedom to Let Go*, Spire Publishing, http://www.hopefortheheart.com/

64. John Egglen and Charles Spurgeon by Max Lucado, www. crosswalk.com/devotionals/upwords/upwords-week-of-aug-11-17-1414475.html

65. Mark Buchanan, *The Rest of God*, Nashville TN: Thomas Nelson, 2007.

66. John Egglen and Charles Spurgeon by Max Lucado, www. crosswalk.com/devotionals/upwords/upwords-week-of-aug-11-17-1414475.html

67. Henri Nouwen prayer, *Harper Collins Book of Prayers*, Edison NJ: Castle, 1997. p. 274.

68. Mark Batterson, *All In*, Grand Rapids MI: Zondervan, 2013. p. 60.
69. Bill Bright, "How To Be Filled with the Holy Spirit," www.cru.org/training-and-growth/classics
70. Arthur Bennet, *The Valley of Vision*, copyright 1975. used by permission of The Banner of Truth, Carlilse PA 17013. "Spiritus Sanctus," p. 27.
71. Mark Batterson, *All In*, ibid. p. 69.
72. Randy Alcorn, "What the Devil Meant for Harm," http://www.cbn.com/
73. Mark Batterson, *All In*, ibid. p. 156.
74. Stephen A. Macchia, *Crafting a Rule of Life*, Downers Grove IL: InterVarsity Press, 2012. p. 125.
75. Walter Wangerin, Jr., *Ragman and Other Cries of Faith*, New York NY: HarperCollins, 1984.
76. John Bradford, "Daily Meditations," quoted in *Near To The Heart of God,* compiled by Bernard Bagley, Wheaton IL: Harold Shaw Publishers, 1998. March 6 entry.
77. Robert Benson, *A Good Life*, ibid. p. 68-69.
78. William Barclay prayer, *The Complete Book of Christian Prayer*, New York NY: Continuum, 2000. p. 834.
79. Robert Benson, *In Constant Prayer*, Nashville TN: Thomas Nelson, 2008. p. 138.
80. David McCullough, *The Great Bridge*, New York NY: Simon & Schuster, 2012.
81. *Book of Common Prayer*, ibid. http://www.bcponline.org/ Daily Office/devotion.html
82. *Book of Common Prayer*, ibid.http://www.bcponline.org/ Daily Office/ep2.html
83. Thomas Aquinas quoted in *Between Heaven and Earth* by Ken Gire. San Francisco CA: Harper, 1993. p. 72.
84. Michael Card, *A Sacred Sorrow*, Colorado Springs CO: NavPress, 2005. p. 11.
85. Michael Card, *A Sacred Sorrow*, ibid. p. 29.
86. Shane Claiborne, Jonathan Wilson-Hartgrove, Enama Okoro, *Common Prayer*, Grand Rapids MI: Zondervan, 2010. p. 471.

87. Ken Gire, *The Work of His Hands*, Ann Arbor MI: Servant Publications, 2002. pp. 85-86.

88. *Ministry of Hospitality Prayers*, www.svfparish.org/page/544

89. *Prayer* by Ken Boa used by permission of the author. www.KenBoa.org/blog

90. Helen Lemmel, "Turn Your Eyes Upon Jesus," public domain. www.cyberhymnal.org/htm/t/u/turnyour.htm

91. Lilias Trotter, "Focussed: A Story and a Song," public domain. http://www.unveiling.org/lily/focussed.html

92. Leighton Ford, *The Attentive Life*, Downers Grove IL: InterVarsity Press, 2008. p. 101.

93. Prayer by St. Anselm. http://www.peopleforothers.loyolapress.com/2013/08/prayer-of-st-anselm/

94. Kurt Bjorklund, *Prayers for Today*, Chicago IL: Moody Publishers, 2011. p. 20.

95. Amy Carmichael, "For Our Children," in *Toward Jerusalem*, copyright 1936 by the Dohnavur Fellowship. Used by permission of CLC Publications. May not be further reproduced. All rights reserved.

96. Christin Ditchfield, *What Women Should Know About Facing Fear*, Abiline TX: Leafwood Publishers, 2013. p. 84.

97. Richard Swenson, *The Overload Syndrome*, Colorado Springs CO: NavPress, 1998. p. 37.

98. Hannah Whithall Smith, *The Christian's Secret of a Happy Life*, 1925.

99. Christin Ditchfield, ibid. p. 87.

100. Teresa of Avila prayer. www.ewtn.com/Devotionals/prayers/StTeresaofAvila.htm

101. Jennifer Kennedy Dean and Cheri Fuller, *The One Year Praying the Promises of God*, Wheaton IL: Tyndale Publishers, 2012. January 8 entry.

102. Madeline L'Engle, "First Coming," quoted in Christian Ethics Today, Volume 10, Number 5, Issue 52, Christmas 2004. www.christianethicstoday.com/PDF/CET_Issue_052.pdf/

103. Kelly K. Lam, "More Stars Found in the Universe," The Harvard Crimson, Dec. 3, 2010.http://www.thecrimson.com/

104. Frederica Matthewes-Greene, "First Fruits of Prayer," quoted by Peter Scazzero in Daily Office, Elmhurst NY: Emotionally Healthy Spirituality, 2008. p. 33.

105. John Henry Newman, *Catholic Prayer Book*, Cincinnati OH: St. Anthony Messenger Press, 1986.

106. Gordon MacDonald, *Mid-Course Correction*, Nashville TN: Thomas Nelson, 2000. p. 235-236.

107. Kate Wilkinson, "May The Mind of Christ My Savior," public domain. www.cyberhymnal.org/htm/m/a/maytmind.htm

108. Claiborne, Wilson-Hartgrove, Okoro, Common Prayer, ibid. p. 298.

109. Jennifer Kennedy Dean, *Set Apart*, Birmingham AL: New Hope Publishers, 2009.

110. Aristides, "The Apology of Aristides: Texts & Stimulus," translation from the Syriac (1891), pp. 35-51. http://www.tertullian.org/fathers/aristides_05_trans.htm

111. Cardinal Merry de Val, 1865-1930, public domain. https://www.ewtn.com/Devotionals/Litanies/humility.htm

112. Charles Swindoll, ibid. p. 78.

113. C.S. Lewis, *The Chronicles of Narnia*. www.goodreads.com/work/quotes/781271-the-chronicles-of-narnia

114. John Calvin in *Classic Christian Prayers*, edited by Owen Collins, New York NY: Testament Books, 1999. p. 151.

115. Joni Eareckson Tada, "From the Heart," Joni and Friends Ministry News, February 2014, p. 3.

116. My home church was gathered in 1635. First Church of Christ Congregational in Old Wethersfield, Connecticut. http://www.firstchurch.org/

117. Lettie B. Cowman, *Streams in the Desert*, 1925. www.youdevotion.com/streams/december/19

118. Stephen W. Smith, ibid. p. 60.

119. Sam Crabtree, "20 Ideas for Encouraging Others," http://www.familylife.com/articles/topics/faith/essentials/reaching-out/20-ideas-for-encouraging-others#. UOrUjVVdVIE

120. Stephen A. Macchia, ibid. p. 103.

121. Joseph Bayly, *View From A Hearse*, Wheaton IL: David C. Cook, 1973.

122. *Book of Common Prayer. The Episcopal Church. New York:* The Church Hymnal, 1979, p. 145.

123. Henry F. Lyte, "Abide With Me," public domain. www.cyberhymnal.org/htm/a/b/abidewme.htm

124. Tim and Kathy Keller, *The Meaning of Marriage*, New York NY: Dutton, 2011. p. 104.

125. David McCasland, Oswald Chambers: *Abandoned to God*, Grand Rapids MI: Discovery House, 1993. p. 238

126. Orthodox Prayer for Marriage www.saintgregoryoutreach.org/2010/01/prayers-for-husband-and-wife.html

127. John Wesley, in *Book of a Thousand Prayers*, compiled by Angela Ashwin, Grand Rapids MI: Zondervan, 1996. p. 24.

Bible Versions and Permissions